TO
EVERY
HAIK

Breath of Life for All

WITH
PEACE

Vic Hummel

MAY 2008

Other books of haiku poetry by Vic Hummert:

- *Tersely Yours*, Volume 1 (1993. 40 pages)
- *Tersely Yours*, Volume 2 (1998. 80 pages)
- *Tersely Yours*, Volume 3 (1998. 92 pages)
- *Walking Humbly with God on Our Wounded Earth* (2000. 64 pages)
- *Breath of Life for All: Haiku Poetry in Defense of Nature* (2002. 102 pages)

Breath of Life for All
Haiku Poetry In Defense of Nature

Vic Hummert

Authors Choice Press
New York Lincoln Shangh

Breath Of Life For All
Haiku Poetry In Defense of Nature

Copyright © 2002, 2007 by Victor A. Hummert

All rights reserved. No part of this book may be used or reproduced by any means, graphic, electronic, or mechanical, including photocopying, recording, taping or by any information storage retrieval system without the written permission of the publisher except in the case of brief quotations embodied in critical articles and reviews.

Authors Choice Press
an imprint of iUniverse, Inc.

iUniverse books may be ordered through booksellers or by contacting:

iUniverse
2021 Pine Lake Road, Suite 100
Lincoln, NE 68512
www.iuniverse.com
1-800-Authors (1-800-288-4677)

Originally published by Vic Hummert
Originally published as Breath Of Life For All

The views expressed in this work are solely those of the author and do not necessarily reflect the views of the publisher, and the publisher hereby disclaims any responsibility for them.

Website: http://vichumert.org

ISBN-13: 978-0-595-43780-1
ISBN-10: 0-595-43780-X

Printed in the United States of America

Acknowledgments

Breath of Life for All is a title chosen for the fifth volume of haiku in defense of nature. *Tersely Yours, I, II, III,* and *Walking Humbly with God on Our Wounded Earth* are the earlier books. The title flows from my two years in Maryknoll Seminary (Glen Ellyn, Illinois, 1960-1962). I am grateful to the late Fr. John McConnell, a highly respected Scripture professor who taught us the ancient Hebrew believers had no word for God other than *r'huah* meaning "the Breath." Our God who goes far beyond human description is the One Source of all life. We live and move only through the Breath that continues to grant each one of us one more breath, still another heartbeat. We are granted more time to pour out gratitude for all that we have received. Yet not all. Most of the people in our crowded world of 6.1 billion are deprived to some degree. For what can they be grateful? If polluted air, poisoned rivers, dying trees and nature could express their gratitude, would we hear anything? Animals on the verge of extinction would perhaps have harsh words for humankind now "moonscaping" Earth and destroying their habitat.

Would island nations threatened by a rising ocean (there is only one body of water that we have given different names) give thanks as we in the United States refuse to reduce our carbon dioxide emissions? The United States still stands in obtuse defiance of thousands of scientists and 178 nations (*The New York Times,* 24 July 2001) by rejecting a treaty to reduce carbon dioxide emissions. Instead of decreasing carbon dioxide emissions, the United States has defiantly been increasing the output by at least 1 percent each year. Global terrorism has numerous faces. The Breath was never intended to be infiltrated by mercury and other deadly heavy metals.

In the twentieth century scientists found mercury in the fish of the Atlantic and Pacific.

Fr. McConnell mixed biblical insights with his gentle humor. When he hastened off to a meeting of professors one afternoon, he invited our class of biblical students to draw the Temple in Jerusalem with all of its various sections. Thomas Shea, a classmate from Boston, who later went back to God at age sixty-one after spending over thirty years of his adult life in Tanzania, drew a small square with the caption: "View of the Temple from 10,000 feet" and handed in his paper to the professor. The following class, McConnell, not to be outwitted, placed a small dot on top of the paper and wrote boldly: "View of a Zero from 10 feet."

My deepest gratitude goes out to John McConnell and other Maryknoll friends over thirty-seven rewarding years (1960-1997) for opening my eyes. Tom Shea and John McConnell summon us to view our Earth from a higher altitude, striving for the macroview of where we are in time. From the decade spent in Hong Kong (where the Mong Kok region of Kowloon once had 400,000 people per square mile), I learned how the Chinese take a long view of history. Sadly, their plunge into a free market economy will sacrifice much of the beautiful terrain and many of their cherished values coming from a 10,000-year-long history.

Now in Lafayette, La., I continue to give thanks for the friendship that began in Hong Kong in 1971 with Dr. Don and Mary Langford, who returned to Louisiana after twenty-six years as missioners in Hong Kong. In 1994 the Langfords invited me here to serve as a chaplain for hospice, then offered me a home away from my family in Breese, Illinois, and Kansas City. They provide information on Scripture passages or the proper spelling of *r'huah* when my biblical knowledge or memory fail. Dr. Langford is the only physician from Lafayette to come out by boldly joining us in public to oppose plans for GTX, the largest toxic waste incinerator in the United States. This "monstrosity," as described by our lawyer Charley Hutchins, was defeated on October 4, 1990 and a second time on Earth Day, April 22, 2002. Environmental victories are not permanent when money and power are symbiotic twins. The waste burner was intended for Amelia, La., a small community with a population that is 47 percent Vietnamese. Our struggle against chemical warfare continues.. The permit for GTX was first overturned in a Baton Rouge District Court in 1999 on the feast day of St. Francis, October 4 . However, Governor Mike Foster, who wants GTX to open, then left this "victory" to the appeals court in Louisiana. As expected, the court of appeals overturned our temporary victory one year later. How odd it is that Governor Foster (whose income in 2001 was approximately $2 million (*The Advocate* [Baton Rouge], January 24, 2002) welcomes this incinerator in a state that has already been inundated by toxins. The toxic air release in the area near Convent, La., is 250,000 lbs. per square mile. The national average is 382 lbs. per sq. mile (U.S. EPA statistics, 1994).

Louisiana has been designated as a "Toxic Sacrifice Zone." It is no coincidence that the most environmentally wounded state in the union is also one of the poorest economically. Thomas Berry's simple insight is hard for people in power to digest: "You cannot have a healthy economy in a sick world."

Following my resignation from the Catholic priesthood, after thirty years, I found myself without a job as the hospice chaplain. The organization dedicated to care of terminally ill patients wanted an ordained priest in an area that is 70 percent Catholic. This rather drastic reversal in our lives occurred in February 1998, just one month before Roselyn Grace Hebert and I were married in the University of Louisiana-Lafayette (ULL) chapel on March 7. March 7 is also Roselyn's birthday.

During my time of unemployment Rose served as a chaplain in Our Lady of Lourdes Medical Center of Lafayette. With no special skills in the job field, computer illiterate, I applied in several schools to tutor failing students. While waiting for steady employment, I took a job carrying out groceries at the local Winn-Dixie market. For those who found this a "degrading" form of employment, I reminded them of my job in a Hong Kong plastics factory in 1972, earning $2.30 for an eight-hour day, bereft of air-conditioning. My purpose was not to earn money but to gain a priceless language experience among young men working in the shipping areas of the factory. The air-conditioned Winn-Dixie store with 10,000 items stacked on a clean floor was indeed a luxury. In 1999 James Rabelais, principal of Broussard Middle school hired me as a tutor in English-language skills and social studies. I taught only those students who were failing or who were too disruptive to remain in a classroom. One lad wrote a thank you note to me and thought I was "the best tudor in the whole world." Then funding for the tutorial program was cut by the school district. I lost two jobs in two years. After offering to tutor in the local county (parish) jail, Sheriff Mike Neustrom hired me as inter-faith chaplain for the Lafayette Parish Correctional Center.

Harold and Sarah Schoeffler continue to provide their kindness and hospitality to Rose and myself. We celebrated our March 7, 1998, wedding reception in the home of Harold and Sarah, driven, not in a stretch limo, but in the pickup truck of Dr. Don Langford. Harold, now head of the Sierra Club, carries on his efforts to preserve a vanishing Louisiana. The area is "tilting" into the relentlessly encroaching Gulf of Mexico. Gulf waters are swallowing the Pelican State coastline at the rate of a football field every twenty minutes. Eighty percent of coastal erosion occurs in Louisiana.

Harold spoke out for the Louisiana black bear and after an eight-year legal struggle had the beleaguered bear placed on the endangered species list. Harold's concern includes other creatures now losing their habitat in this beautiful and neglected region.

Bob Chaney does not tire of helping me through the steps of learning how to use a computer. Often, when telephone directions do not succeed, Bob "abandoned" Marie, then drove to our home and personally put me back on track with technology that is new territory for me. Both Roselyn, my long-suffering wife, and Marie tolerate our commitment to preparing "one more book" of haiku poetry. Hours at the computer means less time spent with Roselyn, who lovingly encouraged me to proceed with this fifth book of haiku.

My deep thanks to Adam Chandler, who grew tired of waiting for the printed word and set up a website for several thousand of my haiku. From his new post as a librarian in Cornell, Adam generously maintains the website–www.vichummert.org–for all to sample. As of May 2002 I have over 5,500 haiku "in the electronic pipeline." These will eventually find their way to the website. Through the website prepared by Adam, the haiku go around the world.

Haiku originated in Japan in the 1700s. Basho is accredited with being the "founding father of haiku," as explained in four previous volumes of poetry. Haiku is a 5-7-5, three-line verse in praise of nature or terse perceptive observations on the awesome beauty of nature. A reader from Japan sent me a harsh email message in 2001 telling me I had "no right to use haiku for my political purposes. Poetry is poetry and should only be written as the originator (Basho) intended." I responded to the Japanese writer: "Basho was surrounded by an abundance of nature, beautiful lakes, flowers, forests, birds, and running streams. He and the other haiku writers could easily compose poetry in praise of nature. However, in our day, all those gifts of nature are vanishing. I have opted to write haiku in defense of a declining Earth. In the next life I will seek forgiveness from Basho." No response was forthcoming from Japan.

In February 2001, Matthew and Benita Stroderd, moved in across the street. Matt has provided more assistance on the computer, which helped along the production of this book.

Not least, my thanks to Linda Calvert of the Mayor's Environmental Affairs Department in New Orleans, who took time from her busy schedule and agreed to read this book in advance, make corrections, and then prepare an introduction.

The Scientific American for October 2000 has a disturbing article about the precarious oceanic possible future of New Orleans, a city already eight feet below sea level. Linda has already made plans to move to safer territory in San Antonio. She will make her contribution there in the field of energy conservation. Her decision perhaps predated the article about threats to New Orleans.

This small book is intended to elevate our collective consciousness and foster a desire to care for creation. In January 1990 Pope John Paul II wrote a pastoral letter entitled "Peace with Creation: Peace with Our Creator." Sr. Susan Mika, a dedicated Benedictine nun, and I were co-hosts on a weekly San Antonio television program entitled *The Sacred Earth*. There were occasional accusations of my being a "new age pantheist." In defense, our Catholic television show began with a bold quote from Pope John Paul's letter: "WE ALL HAVE A MORAL OBLIGATION TO CARE FOR OUR ENVIRONMENT."

The following haiku are spiritual, ecological (how can we separate the two?), autobiographical, and occasionally political. They are written with love for "Pacha Mama" (Aymara for Mother Earth).

My faithful friend and mentor, Thomas Berry (now 88-years-old and retired in Greensboro, N.C.) has been a profound influence in my life. In March 1989 I phoned his Riverdale Center in the Bronx (N.Y.) to ask if we could meet sometime to chat. I simply wanted to meet the author of books or articles I enjoyed so much. "What are you doing for lunch?" asked Thomas. Since I did not own a car Thomas picked me up and we drove to a diner in Yonkers. There I was treated to a stimulating three-hour lunch. Over the past thirteen years I have met several people who are concerned about the environment but unable to find time to peruse Berry's writings. My haiku are humble attempts to capture the ideas of a brilliant "ecological prophet" for others to consider while safeguarding our air, water, and magnanimous ("generous and noble of heart, especially in forgiving injuries") Earth. Thomas thanked me for such an effort in a phone conversation on January 20, 2002. I choose that multisyllabic adjective (magnanimous) because heretofore we have not regarded the planet as our provider and friend. There might be recovery of nature if we change our ways now.

In previous volumes I have referred to Dr. Ignatz Semmelweis (1818-1865), the doctor in Vienna who tried to convince his cohorts to wash their hands after treating a sick patient. He was regarded as mentally unsound for making such a proposal. It took forty years for his sanitary recommendation to be accepted. We do not have forty years to reverse our unprecedented destruction of life on planet Earth.

However, many scientists dispute the claim of Earth's possible recovery. They insist that damage to the Earth is already irreversible. Harvard biologist E.O. Wilson states: "Homo sapiens destroys, Nature will redeem." Wilson believes that "humanity has initiated the sixth great extinction spasm, rushing to eternity a large fraction of our fellow species in a single generation" (*Diversity of Life*, pp. 31-32). Our future in relationship to Earth is not a question of optimism or pessimism; the issue is our depth of love for the planet, backed by our desire to protect the one-time endowment of nature.

Earth is self-healing, and will possibly recover from our senseless activities, if we begin a new history of care for our continual source of life. "Re-inventing the human," as called for by Thomas Berry, is everyone's daily challenge.

We can join doctors who recite the Hippocratic Oath upon completion of their studies by declaring, "FIRST, DO NO HARM."

> Breath of Life for all
> Flows from God through Earth which begs
> For greater respect

Vic Hummert, Lafayette, La.
Martin Luther King Day, January 21, 2002

Introduction

I first met Vic Hummert at a Sierra Club meeting in Lafayette, Louisiana, sometime in 1998. The meetings took place, and I assume they still do, in the area of Lafayette known as the "Oil Center." It is fitting that the local environmentalists would meet in the heart of the oil industry's regional wheeling-and-dealing center. That's Louisiana. There is simply no escaping the dominance of the oil/gas/petrochemical industry. It is everywhere. Struggles between industry- and non-industry-affiliated citizens litter the streets, fields, buildings, and bayous, from Lake Charles to New Orleans, Morgan City to Shreveport. Louisiana is indeed a different place, but it is not the food or music or the humidity that sets it apart.

The relentless war over the fundamental ingredients of life – air and water – adds a dimension to living in Louisiana that I have not seen in other places. A war is being fought, a war between those who favor polluting industries (for example, the governor and secretary of the Department of Environmental Quality) and citizens – courageous individuals who are trying to make the state cleaner and safer for their families and future generations. Vic is one of the heroes who gives others faith that it will be better, some day.

After seeing me at the Sierra Club meetings a few times Vic invited me over for dinner to meet his wonderful wife Rose. The deal was, I would tutor Vic on the computer and in return they would feed me tofu chili or spaghetti or something, followed (of course!) by dessert. I loved being in their wonderful, lively home. Vic and Rose are two of the most beautiful and caring people I have ever encountered. One of my first assignments, I recall, was helping Vic to find some lost pages of poetry on his computer's hard drive (he has a difficult time keeping track of his poetry after typing it in). He carries around in his shirt pocket a small notebook dedicated to storing haiku. After finding the missing files I realized in amazement that he had authored hundreds, even thousands of haiku poems.

Vic's poetry is unique and fascinating. Unlike some, probably most, poets, Vic does not dwell on his individual life. On the contrary, what he writes about is what he sees around him, living and breathing in Louisiana. His haiku have evolved into an interesting hybrid form, somewhere between religious commentary, journalism, and poetry; a righteous burst of spirituality, fact, emotion, and prophecy, compressed into seventeen tiny footnoted syllables.

> We write what we must
> Even defying great names*
> To defend God's Earth†

* Edgar Allen Poe (1809-1840) defined poetry: "Having for its immediate object pleasure, not truth."
† Haiku as intended by Basho, Buson, Shiki, Ryota, Issa, and other Japanese masters, was written in praise of the grandeur of nature. Since the beauty known to them is vanishing fast, if not completely paved over, I chose to write haiku in defense of what remains. We are now locked in the greatest spiritual challenge in history as life for future generations is jeopardized by pursuit of profit.

Quoting Vic's friend and mentor, Thomas Berry:

Haiku is a way of addressing the reality of this situation (ecological decline of the Earth) through the mind by immediate insight. Haiku is cryptic. Its brevity has something of a shock impact of consciousness. It evokes a response before a person can engage in any logical process of apprehension. It provides inspiration before resistance can be activated. Haiku is based on unmediated experience, that is, perception that takes place before the reasoning process begins. This can be considered as instinctive understanding...this immediate awareness we observe in artists, also in parental perception in the needs of children.

(From the introduction by Thomas Berry in *Tersely Yours: Haiku Poetry in Defense of Nature for the Coming Spiritual-Ecological Age*.)

> PHI* was built
> Quite soon to become dead oil's†
> Memorial site (#4808)

* Petroleum Helicopters International (1949-1999, 50th anniversary) is the largest ferrying service of workers to off-shore oil drilling from the rigs in the Gulf of Mexico. A huge office complex was completed near the Lafayette ("Oil City") airport in 2000. Gulf of Mexico oil reserves are compared to those in Saudi Arabia.
† In 1999, Sir John Browne of British Petroleum stood up boldly before energy CEO's in London and declared: "THE AGE OF OIL IS OVER."

Lafayette is more or less a port town (or company town) for the petroleum industry's operations in the Gulf. Helicopters ferry workers and transnational executives out to the ships and rigs offshore. Haiku number 4808 is an illustration of what Vic's best poetry does. At the core lies a prophecy about a time in our future when solar, wind, and perhaps hydrogen power will displace oil. You know, he is right. (John Browne of British Petroleum said it first!) Oil is dead. It is only a matter of time before economics catches up with this truth and when that happens PHI's new headquarters will indeed be a memorial.

I believe in Vic's art. A while ago I created a website so that it would be available to a wider audience, a site dedicated to serving Vic's poetry and to the world: http://vichummert.org. It is not complete. I work on it when time allows. I must say it is sometimes difficult to keep up with Vic. He is a prolific letter and poem writer. It is a work in progress; like a vast garden, I will tend it over the course of my life, until that time in the future that Vic sees, arrives for the rest of us.

Adam Chandler, Librarian,
Cornell University, Ithaca, New York
August 2001

Preface

Vic Hummert is a man of humor, compassion, vision, with the gift of clarity. He honors all of us with his poetry, which is not only a pleasure to read, but the heartfelt truth, uncluttered by the need to impress or be conciliatory.

Vic's haiku speaks to the clairvoyant spirit in each of us, the unfettered essence of who we are and how we connect to each other and to the earth. The rhythm of his words flows from a quiet place where it becomes infused with a radiant energy that makes us smile, nod, and feel true outrage. Carl Jung once said that "the world into which we are born is brutal and cruel, and at the same time of divine beauty." Vic illuminates both this cruelty and beauty in his work, focusing on the divinity of the universe.

In *Breath of Life*, Vic weaves life experiences and current affairs into his fundamental themes of environment, spirituality, injustice, and the havoc wreaked by capitalism: We are now locked in the greatest spiritual challenge in history, as life for future generations is jeopardized by pursuit of profit. He writes intently on global warming and the need to harness the sun for energy. He shares his disbelief over the maneuvering of a toxic waste burning company trying to locate in a nearby town half-full of Vietnamese immigrants. [Written prior to the second victory over GTX on April 22, 2002.] And he aptly brings to bear lessons learned as chaplain of Lafayette Parish Correctional Center, a jail housing nearly seven hundred women and men.

The humanity of this collection is humbling. Many of the verses are annotated with explanations, commentary, and compelling stories from Vic's life. These offer a rich glimpse into the mind of the author, a prophet committed to seek the truth.

A resigned Catholic priest (resignation because of Rome's discrimination against ordination of women), Vic struggles with organized religion: Most religious bodies are lacking in awareness of environmental decline in the present. Yet his earth-centered spirituality is endless: "…survival is possible only if the non-human world is preserved, indeed revered…." He touts the importance of mentors and offers simple methods of meditation that he has shared with the prisoners in the Lafayette parish jail. He reminds us that redemption is still possible if we act NOW:

> When protecting Earth
> Every day is showdown time
> Because we are late

Let us read, meditate, and take action.

Linda S. Calvert, Director
Mayor's Office of Environmental Affairs
New Orleans, La.

A Divine Drama Beginning Billions of Years Ago

What on Earth functions
With greater precision* than
Earth in rotation?

* Earth rotates around the Sun at 648,000 miles per hour (180 miles per second), and has done so with unquestionable precision for billions of years (*The Hidden Heart of the Cosmos* by Brian Swimme, Orbis Books, 1996, p. 53).

In 365 days and 6 hours, Earth completes its journey around the Sun. Therefore every four years a "leap year" is necessary to fit in the 24 hours of a long cosmic journey.

To live is to pray
When gratitude assumes full
Control of our hearts

To love and be loved
In our world of profit leads
All into freedom

Earth will continue
Without humans who will not
Survive without Earth

Wise plans for our day
One hour of deep prayer followed
By God's loving graces*

* "Grace is surprise" (George Bernanos, 1888-1948, French writer, who wrote *Diary of a Country Priest*).

Our demonic forces
Seem most presentable while
Dressed up in rank greed*

* "If it had been the purpose of human history to bring Earth to the edge of ruin, there is no more perfect mechanism than the free market economy" (Kirkpatrick Sale, 1937-).

When speaking pure truth
We need not fear anyone
Plundering our Earth

Return to God's womb*
Occurs at any moment
After our first birth

* Euphemism for death. The second womb is boundless and eternal in giving life to each one.

Why don't we fight* for
Pure air, clean water, good food
As they fade from us?

* If destruction of our air, water, and nourishing Earth was declared a "national security" matter, the forces of survival might be organized in the most challenging moment of our brief history. Compared to the 5-billion-year Earth story, the human event stands alongside as an infant in disposable diapers.

Can we view ourselves
As God sees us each moment
Striving to be loved?

When we have finished
Our share of the race freely
Pass on the baton

At any moment
We have total access* to
Our God who holds us

* We must make appointments just to see the mayor or local leaders.

We write what we must
Even defying great names*
To defend God's Earth†

* Edgar Allen Poe (1809-1840) defined poetry – "Having for its immediate object pleasure, not truth."
† Haiku as intended by Basho, Buson, Shiki, Ryota, Issa and other Japanese masters was written in praise of the grandeur of nature. Since the beauty known to them is vanishing fast, if not completely paved over, I chose to write haiku in defense of what remains. We are now locked in the greatest spiritual challenge in history as life for future generations is jeopardized by pursuit of profit.

Don't ever give up
Because spirit is boundless*
Overcoming all

* "The reality of my life cannot die, for I am indestructible consciousness" (*Metaphysical Meditations* by Parmahansa Yogananda, Self Realization Fellowship, 1964, Los Angeles).

"And who do you say
I am?"* the one model for
All of humankind†

* Mark 8:27
† There are three levels of brain development according to neuroscientists: (1) the reptilian in which we strike like a cobra or alligator; (2) the mammal level, such as observed in our playful, yet capable of growling and snapping, pet dogs; (3) the striving for higher consciousness, to which we are all called.

Our most honest friend
Is the one who reflects God's
Truth personified

Is it the bright light
Or intense heat which makes us
Change our course in life?*

* Sermon given by a trustee at the Lafayette Parish Correctional Center (LPCC) in Lafayette, La., (February 11, 2001) This question applies to the fear of punishment in the penal system and the present anxiety over global warming. In 2000, one person out of every 137 was incarcerated in the United States. The global percentage is 1 out of every 1000. Too many are not "seeing the light," but definitely feeling the heat of prison authorities. Louisiana has the highest percentage of incarceration in the world—800 out of every 100,000, Texas is second with 700 and Russia third with 600 taken from every 100,000. Is there a metaphysical relationship between incarceration and ecological destruction? Texas and Louisiana are the two most environmentally damaged states in the union.

In one century
Fossil fuels will have given
Way to solar might*

* What is lacking only is the political will to accommodate the solar age. Just as John F. Kennedy said, "We will put a man on the moon," a president (not beholden to energy firms) might say, "The solar age is upon us, and we shall follow the light."

We are bound to fight*
Toxic time bombs overseen by
Nuclear weapons

* For the sake of future generations, we cannot ignore this dual threat to all life, human and non-human.

"Los Ricos"* can't say
"Option for the poor"† without
Discomfort inside

* Spanish word for the wealthy class.
† Declarations by the Latin American church conferences in Puebla, Mexico and Medellín, Colombia in the 1960's brought about major changes of consciousness in the Catholic church of Latin America.

One nation* can plunge
All into misery through
Crass selfish interests

* Refusal by the United States to lower carbon dioxide emissions (1/4 of the globe by 5 percent of the people). Please read *Climate Change Impacts on the United States* by the National Assessment Synthesis Team (Cambridge University Press, 2000) and *Global Climate Change: A Plea for Dialogue, Prudence and the Common Good* (U.S. Catholic Conference, 2001). The website www.climatehotmap.com gives a daily update on the effects of global warming.

We don't recognize
Global capitalism
As "mass destruction"*

* There are harsh denunciations of some nations for building weapons of "mass destruction." The Pentagon has plans to design a weapon eleven times more powerful than the 20 kiloton bomb that flattened Hiroshima.

As with butterflies
We all metamorphose from
Earth to fullest life*

* "I will spend my eternity doing good on Earth." (St. Theresa of Lisieux, 1873-1897)

> Population "sinks"*
> Are products of blindness
> Enveloped in greed†

* 90 percent of births in Russia, according to a Russian Orthodox priest interviewed on a Catholic television program, are not healthy (January 2001). There are more deaths than births now recorded in Russia. The highest number of HIV/AIDS patients is to be found in Russia in 2002.

† Although 90 percent of the people in Russia disagree, the Russian parliament voted 320-30 on December 20, 2000 to overturn an environmental ban on the importation of nuclear wastes. The United States will begin shipments of spent fuel to Russia. "The Russian leadership boasts of $20 billion going into their treasury, most going to the notoriously corrupt Russian nuclear agency – Minatom" (*Counter Punch*, January 6, 2001).

> Be not invasive
> When gentler methods can be*
> Employed without harm†

* In healing, doctors who are wise and not seeking personal gain from unnecessary surgeries prefer "not to let the air in." In 1999 my fourth brain tumor was discovered. However, Dr. Karl Jacob, a St. Louis neurosurgeon who removed the third tumor in 1977, advised against the risk of infection, hemorrhage or additional paralysis on my left side. I chose to live in peace with the brain tumor.

†Simply "befriending" our terminal illness and placing our future in God's hands.

> One cannot out run
> Brain tumors, so just relax*
> Then call them friends

* Twenty years after my first brain surgery in 1973, this haiku was written, to be followed by 5,500 more. My niece Vicki Marie Knebel-Davis, who was ordained as an Episcopal priest on May 25, 2002, urged me to prepare books of poetry.

"How much time is left?"
One recurring question from
Searching young people*

* A question regarding "the possible self-inflicted end of history" put forth by a serious male university student to four professors at the University of Louisiana-Lafayette during a pre-election gathering on campus (November 2000).

God's answer to pain
Comes in large doses of morphine
From jeopardized plants*

* Morphine (Morpheus, mythical god of dreams) comes from opium. From January 1995 – February 1998 as chaplain in Hospice of Acadiana, I visited 3000 patients in the Lafayette, La., area, many of whom were recipients of morphine to alleviate their pain from cancer or other terminal illnesses.

May we rest at night
Then raise our bodies calling
No one "enemy"*

* To those in jail I suggest they are spiritually "free" if they do not hate anyone, Government leaders who hate each other, although not incarcerated, are truly imprisoned by their own refusal to forgive and be reconciled.

Our liberation
Flows from absence of any
Inner enemies*

* Others may reject or despise us, but the poison is within them.

We find true bliss when
God provides us with deep joy
Over "jobs to do"

True Ecozoic*
Haiku embrace Earth along
With growth in spirit

* Term of Thomas Berry pointing to the age when our human community will strive for salvation of the non-human world as well as ourselves. Indeed, there is no "wholistic salvation" (body and spirit) apart from planet Earth. Ecozoic haiku are spiritual and environmental messages.

Come Ecozoic
When ecology assumes
Reign over profit

People in quest of
Vanishing frogs* send us clear
Calls to change our ways

* The Fish & Wildlife Department of Louisiana uses volunteers throughout the state to listen for the sound of frogs in the effort to determine how rapid and extensive is the demise of these amphibians.
    CNN of February 6, 2001, reported Indiana initiated the same volunteer program to trace the decline of frogs. We need only recall amphibians depend upon the same biological life support systems as do human beings.

Earth pleads with each one
Protect from all chemicals
Our own DNA*

* Dioxoribonucleic acid is found in the chromosomes of all living cells. Physicist Brian Swimme points out our DNA is now being threatened by infiltration from harmful chemicals (*Canticle to the Cosmos,* XII). Threats to our DNA came as simple scientific facts presented clearly by Rachel Carson in the 1960s.

Shrewd generals know
Our mightiest enemy
Remains tiny germs*

* To this end, Ft. Detrick, Md., is the germ warfare center for the Pentagon.

No one can destroy
Personal relationships
With our loving God

Denial stops our
Age of oil's termination*
As solar awaits

* The United States wishes to prolong the supply of oil by drilling in the Arctic National Wildlife Reservation (ANWAR) and has long-range hopes for obtaining oil surrounding the Caspian Sea. In trying to establish a friendly government in Afghanistan, an effort will be made to run a pipeline through Pakistan and Afghanistan to the Arabian Sea. (Military campaign of October, November, December 2001, purported to be a" war on terrorism.") History will reveal someday, as it did in Pearl Harbor and the deceitful Gulf of Tonkin resolution that people in power have motives that are less than sincere and honorable. Representative Barbara Lee (Dem. Calif.), was the only one of 434 representatives and 100 senators to hold back her support from massive military retaliation in Afghanistan. She later needed bodyguards for protection from those who disagreed with her. She received two thousand death threats after calling for reflection on what we were doing abroad.

Will we run out of
Oil soon enough to save all*
Life on planet Earth?

* Continued burning of fossil fuels (coal, oil, gas) will increase the amount of carbon dioxide in the atmosphere, leading to more global warming and rising of ocean levels.

In every moment
God is striving to touch all
Calling us to peace

With deep compassion
Comes keen sensitivity
To everyone's pain

        Praise shall be heaped on
        Anyone who excels in
        Deep humility

        When the lights go out[*]
        Be still while your true lights shine
        Better in darkness[†]

[*] January 29th, 2001. Winds clocked at 80 m.p.h. struck the center of Lafayette, damaging cars and buildings and paralyzing the Lafayette Parish Correctional Center.

[†] In the darkness and total lockdown for the jail, an eerie silence consumed the facility as no steel doors were slamming, and prisoners were "frozen" in their cells to find their own internal light.

        In their native places
        Prophets are not accepted"[*]
        Because we are blind

[*] "Prophets are not recognized in their own country."(Luke 4:24)

        If grace surrounds us
        We can never turn our backs[*]
        On our God of Love

[*] A woman walked backwards out of St. John's Cathedral on January 30, 2001, obviously not wanting to turn her back to the tabernacle and altar of the church.

        Sacred night music
        Provided by small tree frogs
        Lulls us into peace

        Go tell the "Good News"[*]
        Your salvation depends on
        Care of Mother Earth[†]

[*] The Gospel means "Good News."

[†] Without pure air, water, decent food, our future is jeopardized.

Bob Chaney

> As systems break down
> Waking up is hard to do
> Yet, we can't be still

> Our certain union
> With God's Holy Spirit shows
> In speaking pure Truth*

* "Every truth without exception—and whoever may utter it—is from the Holy Spirit" (Thomas Aquinas, 1225-1294).

> All desire "heaven"
> Few are they who will accept
> Death as its portal

> We shall search in vain
> To know God's very own choice
> Time of our parting

> Nature has no lines*
> Which are perfectly straight, just
> Truth† fixed in our hearts

* "Nature has no straight lines" (Thomas Berry).
† "For me God is Truth" (Mohandas Gandhi). Speaking only truth can be compared to a direct light passing from God through each one to others.

> One alone* can heal
> Unspeakable boredom which
> Grips profit systems†

* Our close personal relationship with God.
† Those who are "nurtured" by the bourgeois mentality of making more money as a goal in life are soon overwhelmed with emptiness by the fleeting, insatiable pursuit of accumulating wealth, power, mansions, clothes, cars, dining in exquisite restaurants.

> There are some children
> Loved from conception* until
> Rebirth in God's womb

* By contrast, many of the residents in Lafayette's jail have been deprived since conception. They are born into homes where both parents are suffering from addictions to drugs and/or alcohol. Too many are born into a violent atmosphere from the first year of life. Frequently, the incarcerated women and men reveal a history of sexual abuse by adults.

> "Marketplace"* is not
> Our primary force in life
> For civilized folks

* We are culturally coded for competition and profit in capitalist societies. We are genetically coded for cooperation and kindness. The essence of our salvation is found in Ezechiel 36:26 where God promises to "remove the stony heart from within and give us a heart of flesh." Working with money as our primary motivation is a facet of the "hard heart." Profit in Hebrew (*besa*) means to "cut or make an incision."

> Dark blackouts roll by*
> While we blindly refuse light
> From our ageless Sun

* Deregulation of energy in California was a failed experiment that brought energy shortages and periods of darkness in California in 2001.

In our pangs of birth
Agony of dis-ease, death
God visits each one

"The greatest nation"*
Is one that cares for deprived
Citizens daily†

* A frequent claim by patriotic, xenophobic politicians and ordinary citizens of the United States, who have never lived in another country. Such blind boasting is tantamount to declaring "cherry pie is the best in the world," while never having sampled another flavor. Costa Rica is one example of civility. In 1948 the government decided to disband the military. This tiny nation has never been invaded. The only threats came from the "contras" which were supported by the United States in an effort to overthrow the government in Nicaragua.
† "Everyone has a right to a standard of living adequate for the health and well-being of his/her family, including food, clothing, housing and medical care and necessary social services, and the right to security in the event of unemployment, sickness, disability, widowhood, old age and other lack of livelihood in the circumstances beyond his/her control." (Article 25 of the UN Declaration of Human Rights, December 1948)

War in our era
Has as its weapons who will
Hate beyond measure

Those who kill for peace
Prefer darkness over light
Drawing blood from God*

* "There is that of God in everyone." (Quaker maxim)

Children must be taught
Words over munitions will
Triumph in God's time

In nuclear times
There will be no ark to guard
Humankind's future

"Warlordism"* reached
Pinnacles of power† seen
Selling arms for cash

* Crude term used to describe Afghanistan's tribal leaders in 2001-2002.
† The five Security Council members (Britain, China, France, Russia and the United States) are the leading arms merchants of the world. The United States sells over half of the world's arms, while the European Union provides one-quarter of the remaining sales of weapons. All of the Security Council members are nuclear powers that have held the planet in the grip of "deterrence" since 1945. The Latin root of deterrence is "to bring fear or terror" into human relationships.

The most devastating environmental possibility is a nuclear war. Radioactivity remains in the soil after the bombing of Hiroshima and Nagasaki August 6 and 9 (1945).

"Our only defense
Against nuclear weapons is
To stop building them"*

* Admiral Noel Gaylor (retired after forty-five years in the U.S. Navy)

We are indeed graced
When jobs are so meaningful*
We can't call them "work"

* October 1, 2000, as chaplain in the Lafayette Parish (county) jail, marked my entry into such a position. No one could feel good at the sight of someone behind bars. The rewards come from trying to help incarcerated women and men find spiritual freedom, along with freedom from drugs or alcohol while serving time. While in jail, some have the first opportunity to find treatment for substance abuse, the first introduction to bible study, and in rare instances, the first time that prisoners feel that someone cares about them! "I will never forget you, chap," said Mr. B, a pilgrim from Paris, Texas, jailed for two weeks after stealing a carton of cigarettes. –"And I didn't even get to smoke one!")

Now is the moment
To leave our nuclear age*
Then move to solar

* "Every institution within which we live today is obsolete because it is pre-atomic in nature." (Dr. William Barry, dean of the Dept. of Education, University of Hawaii, author of *Education for Annihilation*, 1972)

It is an honor
To work for God, not money
As our preference

Learning how to pray
Is our navigation when
In troubled waters

Death is no more than
Our ultimate surrender
To One loving God

God alone can call
Anyone at any time
To leave everyone

Contemplation helps
Our hopes of survival in
Times of real chaos

We don't recognize
Earth alone sustains each one
From cradle till death*

* It is an assumption for theists that God touches each one through the pure air, water, soil, and food that flow from Earth, who is always giving life. Even those in space are "Earthlings," who depend fully upon Earth to survive, as Thomas Berry wisely concludes.

When fear of death fades
Every worry in our brief*
Live will soon vanish

* No hay mal que dure más que cien años ("There is no difficulty in life that lasts longer than one hundred years." Spanish proverb).

Defending our Earth
Is everyone's sacred call
For those who follow*

* Thomas Berry frequently refers to the future of children as a motivation for his lifetime efforts to preserve our planet.

Wherever we are
There will be a platform for
Deep prayer with our God*

* *Hesychia* is a Byzantine tradition of prayer as "stillness or rest in God." This method of prayer was explained by a nineteenth-century author, known only as "the Pilgrim" *(The Way of a Pilgrim,* Harper and Brothers, 1952).

Positivity
Is our best antidote for
Negativity

Pumps, wells will run dry
Sunlight, wind forces will bathe us
In free* abundance

* The universe provides freely. Corporations gather the energy from Sun, fossil fuels or wind then extract exorbitant fees. "Deregulation" of pricing for energy in 1998 has evolved into another market where competition dominates in the relentless drive for profit.

Give thanks for low pay*
Reducing tax dollars that
Buy deadly weapons†

* Such as my own salary. Compared to the 2001 minimum monthly wage of $145 for Cambodians, I am very prosperous. And far more so than the 1 billion people who toil for $1 dollar per day in 2002.
† Nearly half of the U.S. tax dollar goes toward paying for past wars, ongoing conflicts (the Afghanistan war against Taliban was waged at a cost of $1 billion per month) and research for future (R&D) warfare. The Pentagon now has plans to militarize space. A "Space Force" will demand additional billions. In January 2002, the request for another $48 billion was made. The request submitted to Congress was a record $379 billion for the forthcoming year. Lavishing over $1 billion daily to the Defense Department will make us no more secure than before September 11, 2001. But false job security resides with those who are in the "war business."

Superpowers last
Not much longer than Roman
Imperialism

"If you hear God's voice"*
Do not allow distractions
To block such silence†

* Psalm 95
† Silence is the language of God.

> We walk till trails end
> Then with couRAGE* as compass
> Forge a new passage

* Ability to express anger at the violation of Earth generates the couRAGE to act out beyond the ordinary. Julia "Butterfly" Hill chose to protect old growth trees from loggers in California by camping on a platform on top of a tree over one hundred feet above ground. The logging company buzzed the tree with helicopters, played loud music, and resorted to other tactics. For over one year (1999) her nutrition and sanitation were provided by means of buckets that were raised and lowered daily.

> Quails have fled roadsides*
> Driven off by litter which
> Offers no spirit

* Farmers plow their fields right up to the road, leaving no protective cover for quails, rabbits or other small creatures seeking refuge from predators. Removal of vegetation up to the roads allows herbicides to flow directly into ditches which then feed into streams without "purification" by vegetation. Each year, my father would purchase several dozen quail, which we took to the woods in southern Illinois for release and reproduction. I could no longer go out to hunt such beautiful birds as I did in my youth. May 10, 2002, quail were heard in our Lafayette neighborhood, which offers no suitable habitat or protection from feral cats.

> Deep joy in giving*
> Is confidence our gift will
> Be acceptable

* In trying to give something away each day (a compliment, kind greeting, smiles, when not able to give away something tangible) might help us experience a tiny bit of who God is.

> "Don't be unequally
> Yoked"* to those who seek profit
> More than pure service

* "Do not harness yourselves in an uneven team with unbelievers." St. Paul uses a bucolic figure of speech to manifest an imbalance in life. (II Cor. 6:14)

> Preaching the Gospel*
> Without cushions is one means
> Of reducing crowds†

* "Go and preach the Good News, sometimes using words." (St. Francis of Assisi, 1182-1226)
† Often pastors of religious communities are under pressure to build new and larger churches. If the Gospel of Jesus is presented with concrete applications to daily life, many in the benches will choose to ignore the radical message and stay away. Social scientists have proven through numerous studies most people attend church out of obligation and to feel peaceful. If challenges are issued regarding social justice, peacemaking, or care of Earth, many will look for another messenger.

> Gumbel quail resting*
> Along strawberry cactii†
> Take our breath away‡

* A quail bearing a red crown with a protruding feather over the beak, graced with a gray speckled body. This bird is found in western states of the USA.
† Strawberry hedgehog cactus is found in Arizona deserts.
‡ "If the animals were to disappear, we will die a spiritual death" (Chief Seattle).

> "Technique"* of systems
> Will survive only if our
> Earth is held sacred

* Term of Jacques Ellul (1912-1994), a French theologian who described the governing spirit of civilization under either capitalism or communism as impersonal "technique."

> Earth will not sustain
> Continued invasions by
> Enormous autos*

* The Sports Utility Vehicle (SUV) is a sedan placed upon a truck chassis. The gas mileage of such carriages contributes to the uncontrolled release of carbon dioxide into our atmosphere.

Jesus is clearly
God's Compassion shown to all*
Throughout history

* "In Jesus we see who God is and who we are called to become." (Excerpt from a homily given by the late Fr. Bruce Campbell. Maryknoll Seminary, Ossining, N.Y., 1963.)

Upon growing up
We might perceive God's plan for
Our deep compassion

Our goal in this life
Acquiring God's Spirit*
Cannot be purchased

* "Our true goal consists in acquiring the Holy Spirit of God" (Seraphin of Sarov, Russian monk, 1759-1833).

Warmly solicit
Tiny house finches* to our
Homes by any means

* In early January 2001 and 2002 the small birds with red breasts arrived in Lafayette, LA, seeking hospitality.

Write while we have time*
Our angel's embrace hovers
Above us with love

* Our legacy and "children" are found in diaries or books left for posterity.

Protecting forests
In the cenozoic* is
Passing on relics†

* Greek for "most recent" geological period. Industrial plundering is destroying the gift of creation going back 65 million years. Protecting the forests from loggers and exploration for energy will assure the survival of trees that are thousands of years old.
† Mac Hall, a faithful friend from Dallas and "wood turner" (one who works with a lathe, as distinguished from a carpenter) made a pen out of American chestnut wood for me. The piece of wood came from a barn that pre-dates the civil war. At one time, a squirrel could hypothetically journey from the Atlantic all the way to the Mississippi (catching mythical rides ferry rides on fallen trees across broad rivers such as the Hudson and Susquehanna, plus many others too wide for the journey!) and not touch the ground. Now the only American chestnut trees remaining can be found near Lake Travis, Michigan. Because this species of tree has been clear cut, a disease has weakened it. Attempts are being made to cross the tree with an Asian chestnut tree for improving the stock, but it will never be the same tree which once lavishly blanketed the nation.

Florida panthers*
Will find their refuge someday
Only in prisons

* These majestic cats are being driven into extinction by expanding "development" and road construction leading to resort cities. Conservationists fear only 100 panthers remain in freedom. Like many endangered species, their questionable future may be extended for a short while through captivity. Will the zoos hold rituals for the last creature of a species which is about to expire and vanish into extinction?

Desire is our gift
Which draws us ever closer
To God who holds all

We live life forward
While reflecting on chapters
Which passed so quickly

One large falling tree
Did lighten tragedy* in
Taking two lovers†

* It is a rabbi's observation that all marriages end in tragedy because one spouse is taken before the other, unless both happen to die in a plane crash or tragic accident of some other nature.
† In the Christmas season of 2000, a married couple near Lafayette, La., was on the journey to visit friends when a tree, the roots of which were loosened by heavy rains, fell upon their vehicle, taking both at the same moment. The wife had been known to express her deep anxiety as to how she would ever survive if her husband died first.

If we woke up now*
Megawatts of Sun's power
Might warm our cold hearts†

* The Solar age is on the horizon while fossil fuel addicts stave off this certain era for the sake of huge profits channeled through multinational energy corporations.
† A euphemism for stubborn and blind.

Where Earth needs you most
When you espouse deepest peace
Is where God wants you

Utmost honesty
Pouring through human exchanges
Is God within us

> Could it come to pass
> Our whole cosmos was hijacked
> By deceitfulness*?

* Please read *Day of Deceit: The Truth about FDR and Pearl Harbor*. Author Robert Stinnett charges that thirty members of the Roosevelt administration knew about the Japanese attack on Pearl Harbor in advance. The administration was willing to sacrifice thousands of lives in the "surprise" attack leading to a world war that killed 60 million globally. "America has evil men in high places" (William Stringfellow, *An Ethic for Christians and Other Aliens in a Strange Land*, Word Press, Waco, Tx, p. 33).

There are many who refuse to believe the $30 billion annual intelligence operation of the United States did not know in advance of the perfectly timed attack on the World Trade Center and the Pentagon. During May of 2002, disturbing revelations of how much was known in advance of the 9/11 attacks began to surface in the United States. (Please refer to "Bojinka, the Dog that Didn't Bark" (comerupp@silcom.com) for additional background information on September 11, 2001.

> How to win our war*
> On global terrorism
> While losing drug wars?†

* Following the attack upon the World Trade Center on 9/11, the United States declared war upon terrorism. This war will lead us into wars with fifty or sixty nations, according to Secretary of Defense Donald Rumsfeld. Such a prolonged period of warfare could become the equivalent of the 100 Years War, which bled Britain and France from 1337 to 1453. In July 2002 National Public Radio reported, "The United States now has thousands of troops stationed in one hundred countries."

† The ongoing "war on drugs" in the United States, waged since the 1960s has only seen an increase in drug consumption. The movie *Traffic* is a powerful presentation of how such a war has been futile.

> We are unaware
> Of light brought to others through
> Ourselves on dark days*

* "There is no way of telling people they are walking around like the Sun." (Thomas Merton)

"Never say never"
Apart from telling your spouse
"I'll never leave you"

Ill-informed people
Will blindly salute even
Executioners*

* A study of twentieth-century history indicates such a proclivity among those who do not remember world events carefully. "Those who do not study history are condemned to repeat it." (George Santayana, 1863-1952)

Water becomes us*
Pleads through all who drink daily
"Save my purity."

* "When we drink water, it becomes us; and its first thought is that it isn't water. We are over sixty percent water. We are water thinking." (Canticle to the Cosmos, Tape XII, by Brian Swimme)

Vanishing pandas
Fascinating millions worldwide
Black/white face of God

We might spend our days
Going about doing good
Seeking money last*

* "The world would be better off if people tried to become better. And people would become better if they stopped trying to become better off. Everybody would become rich if nobody tried to become richer." (*Easy Essays* by Peter Maurin, co-founder of the Catholic Worker with Dorothy Day in New York City.)

All flowers must soon
Offer their last smile to all
Then return back home

> Our throw-away world
> Has now exhausted LULU's*
> Where no life exists

*Acronym for Local Undesireable Land Usage. LULU's are remote sites in the country where rubbish haulers go to dump municipal solid wastes. The multibillion dollar global waste disposal corporations encourage Municipal Solid Waste (MSW), of which Dr. Barry Commoner warned his students in the 1950s. Recycling programs cut into the multibillion dollar profits of companies that transport detritus from the communities out to beautiful country areas.

City governments, "enlightened" by the infamous Cerrell report used in California in the 1970s, seek communities that will not resist dumping of garbage. Cerrell "experts" suggested

~ poor regions
~ without political cohesion
~ in rural sections, and
~ Catholic

were the best places where dumping could be done without resistance. Catholicism (along with many other denominations) has an excessive amount of "redemption out of this world" theology, which draws believers away from protecting the Earth, upon which we depend. Frequently religious people reject care of Earth "because our home is elsewhere." Most religious bodies are lacking in awareness of environmental decline in the present. Excessive transcendentalism will allow the polluters to trash Earth and profit from the sinful abuse.

After five years of environmental education in Texas (1989 to 1994), with tepid response from the churches there, Fr. Jim Sinnott, a Maryknoll missioner who spent twenty years in Korea said, "You will get no reactions from the churches until ruination of our Earth is declared a sin."

> Complete guilelessness
> Resides only in clear faces
> Of all animals*

*The "human animal" operating from intelligence over instinct, frequently reflects the "performing self" over the true self in personal relationships. Words often mask true feelings and facial expressions do not manifest inner feelings when at parties, weddings or other social gatherings.

Silent prayer will cease
With deepest longing for God's
Endless communion

Earth will not repeat
Her majestic sunrises in
Billions more to come

We will find our bliss*
When life and work are the same†
United in Truth

* The writer/philosopher Joseph Campbell always suggested we "find our bliss" in life.
† Writers, artists, dedicated teachers and physicians, missioners who seek the betterment of those among whom they work are examples of the unification between life, work, and Truth, which is another name for God.

We remain in touch
With eternity* strolling
Lightly on Earth's grass

* 4.8 billion years is the approximate age of planet Earth.

Did we learn to love*
Be loved is all that matters
As we graduate?

* A woman in Lafayette, La., told of her classmates in medical school, 95 percent of whom are divorced.

Clearly our best gift
Is Spirit of Compassion
Flowing now from God

Between Earth and Sun
We all find ourselves transfixed
In the grasp of grace

Earth warns us always
Never dare the edge of steep
One-way waterfalls*

* If global warming and rising ocean levels are certain, how do we know these trends will cease?

Once our great engines
Of false "progress" are released*
Who can slow them down?

* How do we curtail the automobile economy of the United States which has "gridlocked" every city over 100,000 people? Which office-seeker would risk political suicide by suggesting limits to the sale of automobiles? Such a restriction would be tantamount to placing a limit upon profits. "We cannot build our way out of congestion" (an engineer in St. Louis, Mo., *The St. Louis Post-Dispatch,* April 11, 2002).

When Earth's resources fade*
Gouging becomes more intense
Making the poor die

* Columbo-tantalite (Coltan) is a very special mineral that is essential for the manufacturing of cell phones and computers. Coltan is mined in eastern Congo. In order to obtain it, the rain forest is being sacrificed as roving miners dig into the soil. Coltan has jumped from $30 to more than $400 per pound. A nearby national park, once habitat for 8,000 gorillas, now has only 1,000 of the hapless creatures. Hungry miners kill the gorillas for food (*The New York Times Magazine,* August 12, 2001).

Spending many days
Sending love to dear friends
Is our life in God

Basking in God's light
Comes freely to all who have
Turned away from wealth

We are already
Too late to turn systems* back
But we still must try†

* The car economy, militarism, excessive use of throwaway materials now inundating landfills, addiction to fossil fuels, multinational corporate control of the planet are seemingly irreversible.
† When the "Grandfather of the Peace movement," A.J. Muste (died 1967) was ridiculed for demonstrating against World War I, and asked why he was on the street if he knew he would not stop the war. Muste responded, "I will not stop the war by demonstrating, but if I do not act out, I might begin to think like they [those who believe in warfare] do."

Rejecting The Hague*
Nudged global warming on fast
Forward for our Earth

* While the whole world focused on the deadlocked United States presidential race, a meeting on global warming was held in late November 2000 in The Hague. The U.S. representatives were at odds with the European Union and the conference ended in failure. The Hague gathering was a feeble sequel to the Kyoto agreement in 1997, which tried to reduce carbon dioxide emissions to pre-1990 levels. Only six nations in the world generate more carbon dioxide than the state of Texas. As given previously: "178 Nations Reach a Climate Accord; U.S. Only Looks On" (*The New York Times*, Tuesday, July 14, 2001).

When we find our niche
In life there is no "labor"
Just pure privilege

Desperate people
Will purchase pure air bottled
High on Mt. Fuji*

* During my ten years in Hong Kong, one of the many scams I read in *The South China Morning Post* (1972), the leading English daily, was that of a man arrested for selling "Air Bottled on Mt. Fuji" to people in the crowded British colony choking with air fouled by incinerators, vehicles, and factories.

Some make that great leap
Regarding ourselves as Earth
Becoming human*

* We are the Earth taking on consciousness is the radical teaching of Jesuit paleontologist and mystic Pierre Teilhard de Chardin (1881-1955), whose teachings have been carried on by Fr. Thomas Berry (1914-), Sr. Miriam Therese MacGillis, and Brian Swimme, Berry's students.

We have never fought
"War to end war" rather feed
Desires to kill more

We are all from Earth*
Who will try unceasingly to
Give fullness of life

* In the Ash Wednesday liturgy of the Catholic church ministers place ashes on the foreheads of believers with the cosmic words, "Remember, you are from Earth and to Earth you shall return."

"Just simply alive"*
Fills open hearts of millions
With deep gratitude

* Line from a haiku by Issa (1763-1827)

Are we not, each one
Consecrated to our God
In this brief sojourn?

We dine with our God
In moments of gratitude
With hope all will eat*

---

* The reality is 40,000 die daily from malnutrition-related diseases. That is one person dies from malnutrition every three seconds.

Singing while working
Migrants possess more freedom
Than some Ph.D.'s

How do we view Earth
As mother of living things
Or massive market?*

---

* For most of recorded history, nations which dominate have led others in looking upon Earth as the source of resources to be plundered.
After receiving directions from residents in a village, William Butler Yeats (1865-1939), the distinguished Irish poet, posed a question to the townsfolk: "Do you live as a community here, or exist to make money off one another?" This piercing question can be asked of any person, community or nation in the world.

Earth wants us to feel
Her steady decline* inside
Jaws of progress†

---

* Thomas Berry has taught for decades, "The issue now is viability of our Earth."
† Small batteries are regarded as a means to operate without electricity. Batteries contain lead and cadmium which go into the water table, along with harmful acids from the batteries. Car batteries are sold with an additional $1 for the recycling of deadly lead. Jewelers must collect the batteries from hearing aids and watches for special disposal. Each year nearly 3 billion batteries are thrown away by households and hospitals across the nation. When thrown into landfills they pollute our air, ground, and water.

God's unassuming
Silent presence is always
Melting our hard hearts*

* "I will remove from within you the heart of stone and give you a human heart." (Ezechiel 36:26)

"Great economies"
Are not always wholesome for
Children and nature

Servants of systems
Listen more to officials
Than pleas of children

Language is power*
Not expressed by Earth, nature
In courts of lawyers

* Penny Lernoux (1940-1989), the Latin American journalist, noted "God is powerless," until we act on behalf of all who are downtrodden and exploited by the rich and powerful. Penny was so inspired by the Maryknoll Sisters, who worked in Latin America, that she requested to be buried in their cemetery in Ossining, New York.

People of passion
Receive boundless energy
Through contact with God

When our lights go out
Energy sources become scarce
Sun will smile on us

Terminal illness*
Will not crush human spirit
Which flows from God

* December 16, 2000, I attended a graduation party for Joan x, a cancer survivor from Milton, La., who completed her studies in the University of Southwestern Louisiana (now University of Louisiana–Lafayette – ULL).

One Iris in bloom
Thanks global warming during
Sunny December*

* The Iris blooms in spring usually. On December 16, 2001, this beautiful flower was seen alongside St. John's Cathedral in Lafayette, La.

Overheating Earth*
For the first time since "Day One"
Is now occurring

* *The Heat Is On* by Les Gelbspan is a study of global warming.

Earth will protect places*
From exploitation through signs
Of what life could be

* Nature is fighting back through global warming, floods, droughts, storms and other calamities. Vast rain forests, Arctic refuges and pristine beaches are now threatened. The security of such places is voiced through caring human beings and political interfacing with corporations bent on profit alone.

> God remains apart*
> From human idiocy
> Called "religious wars"

* God remains with the suffering victims, but not those who look upon warfare as their means of diplomacy. Nor those leaders who invoke God's name as the battle begins.

> Killing "enemies"*
> Killing in our country rank
> Equal in evil†

* Formerly, people of the Soviet Union were considered as members of an "Evil Empire," a fiction generated by the Defense Department and presidents of the United States since 1945.

† The ethical schizophrenia of history is a value system that incarcerates someone for killing another person on the street, while it offers medals of bravery to a soldier who kills someone declared by national leaders to be the "enemy."

In the Lafayette jail, I visited for many hours with a man who was considered to be a homicidal sociopath. Up to the age of 17 he shot nothing other than rabbits or squirrels near Morgan City, La. When told he would be paid to kill in Vietnam, he became a Special Forces Marine and boasted of accomplishments in the conflict. He felt a return of conscience and was trying to change his life completely. "Rooster" (his prison nickname) left the jail and remains in my prayers that his conscience will develop to the childhood innocence he had before recruiters brainwashed him.

> Why be offended
> When one places union with God
> Over our friendship?

> We cannot claim one
> Original idea when
> All thought is from God

Refusal to kill*
Means prison for those who dare
To follow God's law

* Since the time when Christians refused to participate in the Roman military, throughout the Third Reich when those who refused military service were executed to the present day when conscientious objectors are ridiculed, the wrath of government officials has poured down upon those who oppose militarism.

No matter how wrong
Wretched, we are still children
Of our loving God

Golden meadow larks
Once charming all who drew close
Now seen in bird books*

* Of 9,600 species of birds, only 3,000 are holding their own; the other 6,600 are in decline. Of these the populations of some 1,000 have dropped to the point where they are threatened with extinction" (*State of the World* by Lester Brown, Worldwatch Institute, 1995, p. 4).

Each precious moment
Is pure supplication to
Our God for more life

Our calls for better
Life become more strident as
Earth's good health declines

Good feelings are ours
When we determine to be
Completely sincere

Only with water
Will our human drama flow
Indefinitely

> We live in one world
> Where most exist deprived of
> Very basic needs*

* Those who live in affluent parts of the world find it difficult to accept that the average income for one year for most of the world's 6.1 billion people still remains less than $1000. Professional athletes and CEOs of corporations in the United States snivel at incomes less than several million dollars a year. The football coach of a famed Catholic university will receive $2 million a year. By contrast, in 2001, it is estimated that 1.2 billion people earn $1 per day. In the 1990s there was a national debate in Sweden over the income ratio of executive officers and the lowest paid employee. At issue was the proportion as to whether the CEOs should make four or five times the income of lower employees. Such a discussion would be unthinkable and rejected immediately in corporate offices of the United States. For simplicity, we can speak of belonging in the two-thirds world of the deprived, or the one-third world of privileged and powerful nations.

> Our culture becomes
> More estranged from Gospel hopes*
> With each new weapon†

* Matthew, chapter 5 summarizes expectations for anyone wishing to follow Jesus.
† Every decade the Pentagon must use up old weapons (on chosen weak enemies), then experiment with new widgets (also on the unfortunate countries which are unable to fight against a superpower).

> Our lives are not judged
> "Unproductive"* when God goes
> On transforming us

* Personal transformation occurs especially within prison confines. Sadly, prisons are also a locus of growth in the world of suspicion and lack of trust.

> We will soon judge crimes
> Against nature heinous as
> Those among ourselves

Reinventing time
Requires living for something
Other than profit

Regardless of who
Emerges as our "leader"
We live by conscience*

* Commanders-in-chief have ordered men and women into battle throughout history. In the first three hundred years of Christianity, those who followed the dictates of the gospel refused to serve in the military. Franz Jagerstatter, born on May 29, 1907, was put to death by the Nazis on August 9, 1943, for refusing to serve in the German military after Austria was annexed by Hitler. *In Solitary Witness* by Gordon Zahn is the story of Jagerstatter. The introduction by Reinhold Schneider states:

> "There is no way to hide the fact it is harder to be a Christian today than in the early days of our church. When it becomes 'the sacred duty' of a Christian to commit sin, there is no option other than bearing witness, in solitude. And there we find the Reign of God." (My adaptations into inclusive language.)

God's love is poured forth
Into our hearts to the point
We wish to receive

Life in the Spirit
Means willingness to accept
Unspeakable risks

"In the beginning
Was the Word"* which breathed full life
Into creation

* "In the beginning was the Word: the Word was with God, and the word was God. He was with God in the beginning. Through Him all things were made. Through Him all things came to be" (John's Gospel, chapter 1).

Most of history's
Great civilizations fell
From internal forces*

* Arnold Toynbee (1889-1975) studied the rise and fall of civilizations. He concluded all but three of prominent civilizations in history crumbled from within.

Earth conceived by God
Was immaculate until
Trashed by profiteers*

* Visits to any pristine beach manifest how pure Earth was in pre-industrial years.

Our world of rotund*
Bodies alongside starving
Babies can't please God

* One-fourth of people in the United States are now overweight. A child born in the United States will consume seventy times more than an infant struggling to survive in Peru, Sudan, Nepal, and most recently in Afghanistan.

Engineers deny*
Their world of fossil fuels has
Reached its Omega†

* While returning by air from Dallas on December 9, 2000, I met one engineer from Lake Charles, La., who actually denied the severe pollution problems of this city in western Louisiana. Another employee of Baker-Hughes, a petroleum multinational, would not admit to the falling reserves of petroleum. After working for years in Argentina, he honestly acknowledged 80 percent of the people there were economically deprived, but would not admit to growing resentment by citizens of Latin American nations to pollution left by oil exploration.
† Last letter in the Greek alphabet.

God's Universe waits
With eternal patience
Our awakening

Inhale gratitude
Exhale trust in our loving
God who embraces all*

* As chaplain in a jail, I can only introduce inmates to the possibility of a deeper personal relationship with God. Blocking out thoughts of the past and anxieties over their future, these women and men can focus on feelings of gratitude and trust. "You will come to understand prayer through that simple exercise I have given you" paying attention to the feelings in your body" (*Walking on Water,* by Anthony DeMello, S.J., p. 27). One of the jail residents named Henry T. told of his 20-minute period of silent prayer daily as "the most peaceful time of his life."

Oil magnates seeking
Power* means our addiction†
Will remain for years

* George W. Bush, a Texas oil millionaire, and Dick Cheney, former CEO of the Halliburton Company (with a $20 million stock option and $1.4 million annual salary) won power in the White House in the year 2000. The Republican Party spent over $100 million, another record for the wealthocracy, in their campaign alone. Because of the photo finish between Vice President Al Gore and Governor Bush, millions more were spent on legal fees by the Democrats and Republicans resulting in Republican victory through the Supreme Court thirty-seven days after the November 7 election. George Bush campaigned in Nevada with the promise of "never allowing nuclear waste to be brought to this state." In March 2002, Mr. Bush gave his approval to the dumping of nuclear wastes from across the nation in the Yucca mountain range. One of the angry senators from Nevada appeared on national television the day Mr. Bush reneged on his promise and said, "He lied, he lied, he lied."
† The United States alone imports more than 10 million barrels of oil daily.

Our God and pure Truth
Will be co-identical
At every moment

To "Go the distance"
In Earth healing demands strength
Which nature provides

Petroleum fouls
While faithful solar never
Fails in our new day*

* The Solar Age is upon us, waiting on the horizon 24/7, while energy corporations struggle to protect their huge profits.

One of Earth's hardest
Lessons we can learn is that
Water is sacred*

* "All water is holy" said Prof. Georg Borgstrom in our class on malnutrition in the Third World, taught at St. Joseph's University, Philadelphia, summer 1968.

When heavy metals
Seek to enter lungs of babes
To where do we flee?

We appreciate
Each one of Earth's gifts when they
Are withheld from us

At times we will feel
This is precisely where Earth
Calls us to act out*

* In 1976 a bulldozer was clearing a shack area in Kowloon, Hong Kong. I knew numerous residents had not been registered for alternative housing after their humble abodes would be crushed. I stood in front of the bulldozer and endured cursing from the driver. The blade came within one yard of my feet and halted. After I left, the demolition continued, but a struggle ensued later in which one of the government workers was killed by a resident wielding a large rod. My acting out was a variation on "Don't just stand there…": "Don't just say something – STAND THERE."

It is our hour for
Environmental healing
If we wish to live

God comes to each one
When our hasty breathing* flows
Smoothly into One

* Creatures that breathe slowly live longer.

What gift is more free*
Than God's ever-abundant
Pure Holy Spirit?

* A hypothetical theological argument would pose the question: Must we not work for such a gift? The only "work" necessary is the desire for such an infusion of goodness along with our emptiness leading to the ability to receive.

> A nation that spends
> Billions on defense* deserves
> Nature's rejection†

* During President Reagan's tenure $9,000 per second was spent on the military. "In 2002 the military budget [amounted to about] $700 million per day, $8,000 per second, about $4 a day per person. The money spent on the military is 49 percent of the federal tax dollar. This is more than 22 times as much as the combined military budget of the United States's alleged 'enemies'" (Coleman McCarthy, director of the Center for Peace Studies, Washington, D.C., *National Catholic Reporter,* November 3, 2000). In May 2002, the budget request for the military for the coming year had reached over $379 billion, more than $1 billion per day. By contrast, in 1945 the military budget for the entire *year* was $1 billion. The 2002 figure is sure to go higher. Some critical thinkers regard our military budget in 2002 as the equivalent of a bloodless military coup.

† "The Military and the Environment" is a 30-minute documentary by the Center for Defense Information (Washington, D.C.), a group of retired military personnel who accept defense but warn against our excessive militarism in a nuclear age. This video points out how every military installation leaves dangerous toxic wastes on the site.

> Discussions drag on
> As Earth is plundered daily
> In search of profit*

* Over nine hundred lobbyists choke the hallways of power in Baton Rouge, La. There may be two such lobbyists for environmental groups such as the Sierra Club in the polluted city. As church and environmental gatherings measure out carefully worded documents on protecting Earth, the "busy-ness" community goes forward in search of a simple objective, regardless of the cost to future generations. Recall, (from previous books of haiku) profit in Hebrew is /besa/, meaning "to cut or make an incision."

> Poetry is joy
> When crafted out of sheer love for
> Words over profit

May God help us all
Become living compassion
As our Earthly goal

Do not cast your poems
Before busy people bent
Upon base matters*

* Copies of my collection of haiku entitled *Walking Humbly with God on Our Wounded Earth* were given to a prayer group in Lafayette. Petroleum engineers among them were not pleased with the environmental message it contained.

Who could imagine
Rational beings really
Ran out of water*

* Please read "Running Dry," by Jacques Leslie. The question is posed about the future of humankind when we no longer have enough potable water. (*Harpers,* July 2000)

Impressions we leave
Are the seeds we sow in each
Encounter in life

"Being nobody
Going Nowhere"* may lead us
To enlightenment

* Title of a book by Ayya Kema.

Strive not to crush ants
While walking on hard pathways
Where Earth can't shield them

"Salvation" does not
Mean liberation from tasks
We alone can do*

* No one is indispensable, but it is possible to possess more patience and perseverance than others in caring for someone not necessarily related by blood. Parents frequently give up on an addicted daughter or son and leave them to the care of non-family members. Each one of us knows such a person or persons who find solace from our care.

Any moments not
Fixed on God's surrounding love
Are our distractions

We can limit our
Daily output of poisons
From auto exhausts*

* "Scientists warned that gases from smokestacks, tailpipes, burning forests" will lead to a catastrophic future" (*New York Times,* November 24, 2000). The conference on global warming held in the Hague ended in failure. The European Union was at odds with the United States over proposals to reduce carbon dioxide emissions. There was very limited coverage of the conference by newspapers and television from the United States.

In the United States, not everyone is involved in manufacturing, which emits gas from stacks, nor are we going about setting forest fires, until the late spring of 2002 when individuals were caught doing so in Colorado and Arizona. Most families in the nation own one or more cars. A car that travels 100,000 miles has put thirty-five tons of carbon dioxide into the atmosphere. As explained in previous books of haiku, each gallon of gasoline generates twenty-two pounds of carbon dioxide. This residue is our "atmospheric trash."

Oil consumption in the next twenty years is expected to increase by 54 percent globally (CNN financial news, November 28, 2000).

Rare are they who can
Reflect only upon breath
Coming, then going

We are slow to learn
Nature will never be locked
Under our control

Global computers
Might bring on great crashes without
Spilling human blood

Knowledge with wisdom
Rare gifts that God alone gives
While our world seeks wealth

We teach our children
Never to murder* unless
Presidents want war

---

* Not every soldier is a "murderer," but the soldier must be prepared to kill when called upon. As a most reluctant university (Dayton, Ohio, 1955-57) Reserved Officers Training Corps (ROTC) student, I was taught how to shoot with deadly accuracy (which I already knew from my years as a teenage hunter in Illinois), run through a dummy with a bayonet (and scream to relieve the tension for having just killed someone with a knife), then throw a hand grenade into a building. If any of those deadly actions had been performed outside of the military training grounds, I would be incarcerated. A criminal action on the street can be one of "heroism" when carried out as an order from a commander-in-chief who will not besmirch his own hands.

The Kellogg-Briand Act of 1929, signed by the United States, outlawed war as a means of diplomacy between nations. Presidents in the twentieth century have ignored the Constitutional stipulation that "Congress alone has the power to declare war...."

General Douglas MacArthur told historian Theodore H. White in 1964: "There will be no more wars, White, no more wars...all wars are over." MacArthur realized men like himself were obsolete and war would now be in the hands of scholars and scientists" (T.H. White, *In Search of History*, p. 224).

> Politicians don't
> Know deepest peace that flows from
> Full sincerity*

* Those who speak of peace in our time must change their biblical convictions on peacemaking to vote for an outmoded weapons system which is manufactured in their district or lose votes from constituents.

> Civilizations
> Endure two centuries then
> Crater from within*

* When the thirteen colonies were still a part of England, Professor Alexander Tyler wrote about the fall of the Athenian republic over two thousand years previous to that time:

> A democracy cannot exist as a permanent form of government. It can only exist until the voters discover they can vote themselves money from the public treasure. From that moment on the majority always votes for the candidates promising the most money from the public treasury, with the result that a democracy always collapses over loose fiscal policy followed by a dictatorship.

The average age of the world's great civilizations has been two hundred years. These nations have progressed through the following sequence:
   from bondage to spiritual faith,
   from spiritual faith to great courage,
   from courage to liberty,
   from liberty to abundance,
   from abundance to selfishness,
   from selfishness to complacency,
   from complacency to apathy,
   from apathy to dependency,
   from dependency back to bondage" (A. Tyler).

Earth has harsh limits
On pure water, air to breathe
For living creatures

We must soon enter
Withdrawal symptoms from oil
Addictions worldwide

Even when justice*
Is called "lost cause," we cannot
Give up the struggle†

* Earth Justice is a great threat to the profit system.
† In the early 1990s residents of Waxahachie, Texas (near Dallas) turned back an $11 billion Superconducting Supercollider (SSC) that would have hired 800 scientists. Efforts to block the collider were considered futile, but residents knew of the impending threat from nuclear waste. The Department of Energy tried to deceive the people, but truth won out as the SSC was shut down after Congress squandered $1 billion on the project. There remains a huge hole in the ground near Waxahachie, which might now be useful for growing mushrooms in its darkness.

Until we wake up
Bottled water companies
Will sell what is free*

* At one point in history rivers and smaller streams were potable. Now they are the sources of deadly illness. In 1983, while strolling in cold waters of the River Jordan, I bent down, cupped my hand and drank pure, free water. The industrial society has compromised itself and traded health for profits. It is most unlikely that any major river will be returned to its pristine state of purity in our era bent upon prosperity. And hence, bottled water will be available only to those who can afford such a luxury.

Wherever we go
God holds us all like loving
Parents of newborns

Share what you have now
Opportunities to give
Might not come again

Squirrels cavorting
In loblolly pine trees*
Bark at passers-by

* Species of pine tree with thick bark. That tree is common in Louisiana.

Our spiritual life
And ecological ways
Are interwoven

From five million folks
To six billion in short time*
Burdens our mother

* 10,000 years ago, there were approximately five million people on Earth. In 2000 the population went beyond 6 billion human beings.

Regardless of wars*
Stars still glow with pardon for
Our bloody blindness

* In 10,000 years of history, over 8,000 wars have been recorded. Historians record only 200 years of relative peace for humankind.
"For America (*sic*, [United States of America is the proper term]), there are only two kinds of years – the war years and the interwar years" (George Will, *Newsweek*, 1 October 2001).

Our desires to love
Cherish all is a blessing on
Occasions burden*

* "But I say to those of you who are listening: Love your enemies and do good to those who hate you, bless those who curse you, pray for those who treat you badly."(Luke's Gospel 6:27-29)

>   Ph.D.'s don't know
>   Basic facts about daily*
>   Needs for survival

* Ph.D.'s devoted to opening GTX ,the largest toxic waste incinerator of the United States in the Amelia, La., area were oblivious to the certain pollution of surface water near the site of burning of hazardous materials 24/7. The air and water upon which thousands depend will be sources of poor health if the plant is permitted to function. Profiteering is one of the major causes of pollution globally.

Two victories over this "monstrosity" (description of lawyer Charley Hutchins) on October 4, 2001, and April 22, 2002, mean that the plant will be foisted upon some other impoverished area of the nation. Handling and recycling of toxic wastes will someday be parallel to management of household garbage.

>   The highest good we
>   May realize in our time
>   Is love of others*

* Such is the conviction of Russian novelist Leo Tolstoy (1828-1910).

>   Those who foolishly
>   Declare "God is with us"* are
>   Probably quite lost

* In the 1930's Third Reich members wore large belt buckles which stated: "Gott mit uns" (God is with us)
A videotape of former U.S. national security adviser Brzezinski telling those who fought against the Soviet Union before its demise in 1989 "God is on our side" (*Counterpunch,* November 1-15, 2001, p. 5). In the post-September 11 patriotism, the nation is awash in "One Nation under God" banners.

By biblical standards, God is with the oppressed, poor, and suffering classes of humankind.

>   Wherever God calls
>   Each one to move nobody
>   Can block our pathway

Incineration
Assures everyone will breathe
Poisons round our world*

* February 19, 2001, the Philippine Senate in Manila passed legislation that bans incineration in the nation. The United States lags behind a struggling Asian nation in protecting its citizens from incineration of toxic wastes.

Let us save good soil
Never before tainted by blood
Of humans at war*

* Frozen polar regions have been exempted from our organized mass violence.

We just plant small seeds*
Offering encouragement
Then wait for harvests

* In 1984 I was writing and explaining the Chinese character for faith, trust, or belief (a person standing next to her/his words) to an eighth grade class in an inner-city school of Philadelphia. One student in the Catholic grammar school was so taken by that one word that he went on to gain a Ph.D. in Chinese studies at Temple University. It was not my intention to encourage studies in the Chinese language that day. In the violence that grips our cities, I wanted to emphasize that during my ten years in Hong Kong, I did not witness one fist fight. I often taught a Chinese adage: "Use your mouth (for dialogue), not your fist."

Our micro planning
Is irrelevant unless
There is macro thought*

* Awareness of the Toxic Time Bomb, the nuclear threat and global warming are cosmic backdrops to every human endeavor.

In our large cities
Roaring sounds of the sea are
Millions of autos*

* In 2000, the United States with 275 million people enumerated over 200 million cars and trucks. In 1914 (year of Thomas Berry's birth) there were just 1 million cars in the United States. Life near any expressway brings with it the unnatural burden of a continual sound of cars and trucks rolling by. We then add to the noise one-half of urban air pollution.

Swivel chairs of high
Voltage* will surely bring down
One week of Mondays†

* Euphemism for those who sit in executive positions.
† Indirect manner of describing a day with much stress.

Imperialists
Will certainly follow Rome
In steady decline.

Taking to the streets
Is the choice left for oppressed
People without wealth*

* "In this important venue—the courts — wealthy corporations are now holding all the cards and the traditional environmental movement is powerless to stop them" (*Rachel's Environment & Health Weekly*, no. 732, August 30, 2001).

In Latin America, a popular nonviolent form of social protest is to beat on pots and pans. Such a nerve-wracking din penetrates the corridors of power where the economically poor have no voice. "Falling arms" is

Bob Chaney

a form of economic slowdown that lets the ruling class know their privileged life will not continue if the working class opts to let their weary arms relax. In Hong Kong the "go-slow" protest is a means of gaining attention from the ruling class.

    Which of your treasures
    Must be packed in the casket*
    When God calls you home?

* "The casket has no side compartments" (Chinese proverb).

    Each square mile of Earth*
    Strives daily to recover
    From years of abuse

* "Curtis Travis and Sheri Hester, two researchers from Oak Ridge National Laboratory (ORNL), have just published a study of chemical contamination of planet Earth and have confirmed what many people already know–the entire surface is polluted. What separates Travis and Hester from other U.S. government researchers is their stated belief all this pollution is taking a toll on human health." (*Rachel's Hazardous Waste News*, no. 234, May 22, 1991) *Rachel's Environment & Health Weekly* is the new title of a most valuable resource for anyone concerned about the environment. The Annapolis, Md., publication is not expensive. (410) 263-1584. Email: erf@rachel.org.

    More than politics
    Prayer is the art of every
    Possibility*

* Variation of "politics is the art of the possible."

    Sunlight touching us
    Took twenty thousand years*
    To warm all on Earth

* Sunlight we experience today took eight minutes to travel millions of miles before reaching us.

Whoever kills dies
In conscience before striking
Any fatal blow*

* "Whoever kills, dies himself" (Gustav Landau, 1870-1919).

Being trustworthy
Our compliment greater than
Being loved by all

When immersed in love
We have been set totally
Free to be in God

Only with water
Will our human drama flow
Indefinitely

It cannot make sense
Fighting over oil noting
Water's importance

People of deep faith
Will worry about nothing
While praying always*

* "Worry about nothing; pray for everything." (Philippians 4:4, New Living translation, Wheaton, Ill.)

In times of famine*
It is simply privilege
Just to eat today

* Nearly 1 billion people in 2002 are deprived of adequate food.

Fresh air, water, space
Vanishing before our eyes
Beg us to wake up

Contemplatives might
Maintain deep inner peace while
Old orders crater

We dance, sing, drink, dine
While our soil "tilts"* each moment
Into Mexico

* The Louisiana coastline flows into the Gulf of Mexico at the rate of a football field every twenty minutes. 80 percent of coastal erosion in the United States occurs in Louisiana.

Being kind always
Is our "job skill" beyond reach
Of universities

Are business folks
Simply glorified hawkers*
Cum† college degrees?

* In Hong Kong during the 1970s the hawker economy numbered over 60,000. Hawkers are respectable people who buy a case of oranges for $10 then sell it on the streets for $12. Some with less respectable reputations will stamp Sunkist on each orange and sell the produce for a higher price! In the 1970s those who opened up shop on crowded sidewalks were squeezed by "bent" police officers and could be seen racing down narrow pathways to escape the government officials from the Hawker Division of government, or police in pursuit of "tea money."
† Since Latin is no longer studied, "cum" means" with."

Just who would believe
Small plankton daily provide*
Oxygen for all?

* Some scientists estimate over 75 percent of Earth's oxygen supply comes from ocean-going plankton. Widening ocean pollution leads to plankton die-off.

How far must one walk
In vain to hear "chitchit twee"
Of rare nuthatches*?

* A small lively bird similar to the titmouse and creeper, found in the Northern hemisphere. Like hundreds of species of birds, the nuthatch is rarely seen as bird habitat is destroyed.

Vanishing frogs must
Rejoice when sparse rain drops
On their sun-scorched skin

Our "Great Work"* right now
Is waking up to the pleas
From Earth to reform

* *The Great Work*, title of Thomas Berry's book published in 1999.

Negative thinking
Unless against unjust scenes
Is no source for life*

* On the contrary, anger at injustice, rage at plundering of our planet are true sources of energy. While in Hong Kong (1970-1982) I worked closely with Mrs. Elsie Elliott-Tu. Elsie is known to everyone living in the former British colony. She served as a missionary in China until 1950, then came down to the colony as a British subject. Over 100 people a week came to her small Urban Council office for assistance in all types of problems. Her anger at the injustices experienced by people on the bottom was a source of energy driving her to work 18 hours a day well into her 70s. She remains in Hong Kong as a retired educator, political figure, and faithful friend who personifies integrity.

Treasure of sacred
Silence abounds in forests
Free from moonscapers

When "heart speaks to heart"*
We are surely led by God
To be authentic

* Motto of John Henry Newman (1801-1890).

Noble, unselfish
Actions denote a worthwhile
Life for humankind

Cake with carnivals*
Will keep millions distracted
From real life issues

* Include sports mania and the addiction to inane television programs.

Feeling Your deep peace
Constitutes sufficient proof
God is everywhere

Our staying outside
All day in contact with Earth
Renews one's spirit

It is surely wrong
To drive our non-human world
To oblivion*

* Peter Raven, director of the Missouri Botanical Garden in St. Louis, Mo., points out there are more endangered plants than animals in our era.

Peasants* who are lost
In deep prayer need no other
Proof of God's presence

* "How happy are the poor in spirit; theirs is the Reign of God" (Matthew 5:3). While living in Harlem, Hong Kong, and Latin America I was deeply impressed by the economic poor who sat or knelt in churches, absorbed in prayer, totally unaware of my watching them from a distance. And praying that I might become as they are.

God's life comes daily
Through bodies which manifest
Images of love*

* In addition to our being Earth coming to consciousness (Teilhard de Chardin's radical teaching in the twentieth century) we are personally members of the living body of Christ in history. Only through our lives of giving, serving, loving, is the presence of Christ to be perceived daily.

We can learn from Earth*
Meaningfulness comes through lives
Determined to give

* God and Earth are continually giving fullness of life to us.

> Total dependence
> Prompts us to regard each date
> As special Earth Day*

* Usually the 22nd of April.

> It is hard to pray
> For enemies* when we have
> No one to despise†

* "Love your enemies and pray for those who persecute you" (Matthew 5:44). If someone regards us as an enemy, the hatred and poison reside in their hearts. It is our freedom to rise and retire without calling anyone an "enemy."
† "We will deny you an enemy" (Mikhail Gorbachev, upon realization that the arms race was bleeding and destroying the Soviet Union). Will the one remaining "Superpower" acquire such an awareness?

> God wants with each one
> Communion making all else
> As nothing but dreck*

* When Thomas Aquinas (1225-1274) the great scholar was on his deathbed he remarked about his many writings: "They are to me no more than a bundle of straw."

> If there is a choice
> Between conscience or job loss*
> We must heed "the voice"†

* If we are alert and unfettered by material concerns, "the voice" usually says "Do this" or "Do not move on that issue."
† Biologists in Louisiana were fearful for the future of wildlife in the Atchafalaya basin area if the largest toxic waste incinerator in the nation would open. However, they were more fearful of losing their jobs if they came out openly and opposed the burner and the governor who wants it. Ultimately, the incinerator itself was the loser on Earth Day 2002. What remains is–The Death of GTX celebration.

We must continue
Struggling to protect besieged
Earth for children

Stallions of science
Have broken out of the barn
Destined for dead ends*

* "60 Minutes" reported on cloning of human beings (March 12, 2001).

As fresh water fades
Humankind makes strides in space
Neglecting our home

Earth is God's body*
We the Corpus† of Jesus
For those who have faith

* Theologian Sally MacFague elaborates on this theology in her important book entitled *The Body of God*.
† Latin for "body."

The only killing
Acceptable to God was
A crucifixion

We are too busy
Making money to notice
Our wells* going down

* Hydrologists estimate over half of the United States citizens depend upon ground water daily.

It is our wisdom
Not fear that leads us to walk
Away from conflict

Earth will never die
Our mother is at a stage
Where she gives less life*

* The Physical Quality of Life Index (PQLI) merits as much concern as the Gross National Product (GNP) of any nation.

Immature leaders
Propel our speechless Earth to
Perilous fast flush

Earth calls us to teach
Where you stand is "holy ground"*
In every moment

*"Take off your sandals, for you are standing on holy ground" (Exodus 3:5).

States wrongly presume
They have the right to take lives*
Often in error†

* There is a growing global momentum to call moratoriums upon and eventually ban the death penalty. Illinois placed a moratorium on the death penalty in 2000. Maryland did so in 2002.
† Please read *An Ethic for Christians & Other Aliens in a Strange Land,* by William Stringfellow, the Episcopal priest and poverty lawyer in Harlem in the 1960s. Stringfellow's controversial book is a classic scriptural analysis of social structures in the United States (Word Books, Waco, Texas, 1973).

Homo Sapiens*
Replaced by craving homo
Economicus†

* A survivor of the genus homo sapiens (from the Latin meaning intelligent or thinking).
† A consuming economic creature, "Born to shop" and who "Shop till we drop."

"Got nowhere to go."
Never applies on our path
To a loving God

We live through mentors*
Who open our eyes to Earth's
Most bountiful gifts

* As my eyes were opened to the gifts of Earth by my father Victor Joseph, and his hunting friend, Herman Tebbe, during my childhood, Dr. Georg Borgstrom for me in 1968, Elsie Elliott-Tu in the 1970s, and Thomas Berry since 1984, when I began reading his writings, then more profoundly since meeting Thomas in 1989.

"And the band played on"*
While running short of fresh air
Pure water, good food†

* While the Titanic was sinking, music continued in the ballroom.
† In Louisiana, Baton Rouge air has been known to eat the paint from cars. The Mississippi is polluted from drainage originating in twenty-four states above Louisiana. Although Cajun food is excellent and restaurants abound, what is the impact of tons of chemicals sprayed upon fields and food consumed in south Louisiana? The toxic air releases in some parts of the state – it demands repetition – reach 250,000 lbs. per sq. mile (near Convent, La.), as compared to the national average of 382 lbs. per sq. mile. Louisiana continues as a "Toxic Sacrifice Zone"; likewise Nevada is a "Nuclear Sacrifice Zone."

Sooner than later
God says: "You have loved enough."
Then takes us back home

Hearts of gratitude
Never grow weary of thanks
To the Source of life

Convenience forces
Each one to bear nightly noises*
Endless pollution

* In 2000 Federal Express selected the Greensboro, N.C., airport as its hub for approximately 30,000 yearly take offs and landings between 12 midnight and 5 in the morning. The hundreds of residents who are fighting this plan have all benefited from overnight mail deliveries at some point.

How can we plunder
Earth who gives us all we need
To survive daily?

Mindful of our needs
For this moment before us
We find gratitude*

* Anxiety comes from dwelling on the past or projecting too far into the future. When desires for the non-extant future or past overcome the basic needs of our present moment, anxiety rises.

Our rising above
Where we are now determines
True resurrection*

* Scripture scholar Fr. Barnabas Ahearn taught 90 percent of the resurrection occurs in this life as we rise above sin, selfishness, and insensitivity toward a new consciousness.

To where are we called
In God's vast universe while
Occupying space*?

* "Not to encumber this earth—No pathetic Excelsior, but just this: not to encumber the earth" (Dag Hammarskjold, *Markings*, p. 66, the private diary of the former secretary-general of the United Nations). Through reading this beautiful memoir, I encountered the fascinating haiku poetry style in 1966. Hammarskjold's haiku begin on p. 175. Some examples (although not strictly adhering to the 5-7-5 structure):

"My home drove me
Into the wilderness
Few look for me. Few hear me" (p. 180)

"When the gods play
They look for a string
That has never been touched by men" (p. 189)

"May I be offered
To that in the offering
Which will be offered" (p. 189)

Most animals sense
Humans are prone to kill them
Just to gain cheap thrills

Big showdowns* are here
Between defenders of Earth
And those who plunder

---

* After issuing *Renewing the Earth* in 1993, the $4.2 million effort by major religious denominations to raise care of Earth to a higher priority, *The Wall Street Journal* was quick to perceive that an effort on the part of major Christian denominations and other religious bodies to come forth in defense of Earth would be an eventual obstacle to unbridled growth in the profit system. The *Journal* wrote a critical editorial following publication of *Renewing The Earth*. It is clear that love of Earth's life-giving resources, the air, water, and sources of decent food will be a greater "threat" to the global profit system than socialism or communism.

Bob Chaney

> Deep peace felt in prayer
> Is but a shadow of bliss
> Which God longs to give
>
> Prisons are steel tombs*
> From which God desires to raise
> All to a new life†

* Incarceration is a final resort for parenting that did not take place in one's life. However, since the time of Jesus and earlier, innocent people have been locked up by state authorities who resented the exposure of truth by those who spoke out for justice, peace, and preservation of life.
† In my jail ministry, I have met dozens of men who admit they found a completely new life after the pain of incarceration. "This is the first time I've had an opportunity to read the bible." "This is the first time I've had professional help to deal with my drug/alcohol problem." "This is the first time I felt somebody really cared for me." acknowledged a female resident. Many of the guards are truly caring people.

> Each week is holy*
> To any person who holds
> Our desired Third Eye†

* The days leading up to Easter in Christian calendars are known as Holy Week.
† Until we see with more than two eyes, blindness is our fate. Our "third eye" connects with the heart, bypassing our head.

> God can not approve
> Killing for one's country when
> Other means bring peace*

* We lack a cadre of peacemakers who are willing to exert the energy for peacefulness equal to that effort which goes into organized mass violence.

> Suicide bombers
> Feel desperation beyond
> All definitions

> We have permitted
> Agents of Armageddon*
> To assume power

* Means *Har Megiddo* – Revelation points prophetically to the mountains of Megiddo where the final battle will be fought between the great armies of humankind (Revelation 16:16). Megiddo is a symbol of military disaster. At this location in Israel, the visitor can walk down a stairwell that passes through sixteen levels of destruction. Each time the city was demolished by an enemy, it was rebuilt with the same foolish notion of being impenetrable (Daniel 12:1). In the twenty-first century, nations still absurdly believe that nuclear weaponry is their means to total security.

> Possessing deepest
> Compassion is "expertise"*
> Outranking any

* Fr. Richard Rohr has read widely in the field of neuroscience. He points out that 10 percent of the brain is sufficient to gain a Ph.D., become a doctor, a priest, or a senator. Of what use is the remaining 90 percent? In this part of the brain one finds the biblical gifts of mercy, compassion, forgiveness – all gifts that cannot be gained in the best universities.

> Nature and Spirit
> Fill our souls with peace beyond
> All comprehension

> No matter how steep
> Climbing cold mountains of Truth
> Is our lonely choice*

* Pursuit of Truth leads to occasional loss of friends, jobs, and respect from family members.

> God calls us to be
> With others not through ideas
> Rather from our hearts

> Lacking cosmic views*
> Our practical perspectives
> Will not serve too long†

* Viewing history in terms of seven generations – at least. This wisdom is held by native American groups.
† The choice of obtuse people to cling to fossil fuels will bring about more ecological disasters. "Our economy will suffer" if we change our patterns, argue the CEOs and politicians of the present.

> Global survival*
> Is history's most urgent
> Need in this moment

* "There is now only one issue before us, the issue of survival, not merely physical survival, but survival in the world of fulfillment, survival in a living world, where the violets bloom in the Spring time, where the stars shine down on all in their mystery, survival in a world of meaning. All other issues have dwindled in significance whether in law or governance, in religion, in education, in economics, in medicine, in the arts, these are all in disarray just now because we told ourselves, 'We see!' Our guilt remains" ("The Universe as Sacred," an article of limited circulation, by Thomas Berry, January 1, 2001, Greensboro, N.C.).

> Endless quests for Truth
> Will bring sure crucifixion
> By those in power*

* Throughout history, prophets have been put to death by those who resist truth.

> Money buys power
> Power directs money with
> Plans for more money*

* The Medici family of Florence ruled from 1431 until dying out in 1737. Their ambition was expressed in their coat of arms: "Money to buy power, power to control money."

> Truth must rise again
> When conscience awakens in more*
> Sleepwalking people†

* "Conscience and conscience alone will turn the world on its head"(Bernard Malamud, 1914-1986, novelist from the United States).
† The essence of Buddhism is "to wake up" and be enlightened.

> Ninety percent* of
> Humankind does not suffer
> Great burdens from cars

* For 6,000,000,000 people, there are 600,000,000 vehicles in the twenty-first century. Millions who do not have private cars (nine-tenths of humankind) desire to own one, not fully aware of the constant threat of death or serious injury, the cost of fuel, upkeep, insurance and the collective burden upon society as roads invade neighborhoods while destroying the countryside. Forty thousand people die yearly in the United States from car accidents.

> When up to our chins
> Toxic wastes must find victim
> Zones for disposal*

* Recall the $20 billion paid in 2001 by industrial nations to dump nuclear wastes in Russia. How can this offer differ from a bribe?
  Nevada and New Mexico are becoming the "Nuclear sacrifice zones" of the United States as the burgeoning tons of radioactive wastes must be disposed of. Struggles which lasted decades have been in vain as the Energy Department overwhelmed public opinion. Idaho used the state police to stop incoming shipments of nuclear waste in 1988. In addition to the rebellion by Idaho and Nevada, South Carolina has joined the states in defiance of the Energy Department (*New York Times,* April 12, 2002). Which state would allow something so deadly as nuclear wastes to be brought in to harm the people? July 9, 2002, the U.S. Senate voted in support of making the Yucca mountains Waste Isolation Pilot Project (WIPP) the repository for 70,000 tons of nuclear waste. George Bush campaigned in Nevada with the promise of never allowing nuclear wastes to be dumped in Nevada. Germany opted in 2000 to discontinue nuclear energy over the coming decades.

> Education which
> Sparks life's curiosity
> Might be called worthwhile*

* "If after completing our formal studies, we do not have the desire to read and study for the rest of our lives, then our education has been a failure" (*How To Read A Book* by Mortimer Adler). Adler was an educator from the University of Chicago who designed the Great Books reading program which offered a degree to anyone who read the best books of Western civilization.

> Since we did not ask
> To come to be, gratitude
> Flows from — that we are

> Imagining some
> Of what we already know
> Might bring about changes*

* The extent of global warming in 2000, melting of the polar ice and rising of ocean levels, disappearance of topsoil, desertification, climate change — all are impacting island nations along with 60 percent of human beings who live in coastal regions. Furthermore, the chemical infiltration of our DNA will "bio-accumulate" in generations still to follow. After studying *Silent Spring* by Rachel Carson (1962) and *Our Stolen Future* by Theo Colburn (1998) we realize the extent of chemical "warfare" upon innocent people. *No Immediate Danger* by Dr. Rosalie Bertell (1985) provides our prognosis for a radioactive Earth.

> Freedom consists in
> Total handing over our
> Lives to God's designs*

* Such a position is similar to a "quietism," advocated by a Spanish priest Molinos, who published a *Spiritual Guide* in 1675. By contrast, the prophetic Jesuit priest Daniel Berrigan (1921-) declares, "action is the most explosive dimension of contemplation." Freedom in the Spirit is far from passivity in the political and environmental struggles of life. For many of Berrigan's eighty adult years, the Jesuit priest has been a prophetic voice in the world.

> We cannot remain
> On the quiet mountain when
> People are in need*

* Raphael (1483-1520), the Italian Renaissance painter, captured both the Transfiguration of Jesus (Mark 9:2) and the following occurrence requiring cure of an epileptic (Mark 9:14) in his masterpiece entitled "Mountain of Vision, Valley of Need." Peter, James and John wished to remain on the mountain while nine other apostles struggled at the foot of the peak with a young boy's illness. Escapism was not a realistic spirituality as Jesus refused to linger in the "epiphany," or manifestation of his divine powers on the mountain peak.

> We are "breathing down"*
> Ice† which must flow on frozen
> Immobile cities

* Global warming in the twenty-first century. Ocean levels rose one foot in the twentieth century. Human activities are reversing the geological unfolding of our cosmos.
† "By the breath of God, ice is given and the broad waters are frozen." (Job 37:10)

> When protecting Earth
> Everyday is showdown time
> Because we are late*

* In the 1960s a Peace Corps official for Latin America had a sign in his Washington, D.C., office stating: BE BRIEF, WE ARE ALREADY 25 YEARS TOO LATE.

> Living for giving
> Rather than "ill-gotten gain"*
> Makes us one with God†

* *Popular Fallacies*, written by Charles Lamb (1775-1834).
† Whose nature is simply to give life.

Earth cries out to us
"You cannot be sustained much
Longer in your ways"

Can we stop our clock
When seventeen species* leave
Every precious hour?

* Estimated number of species falling into extinction each hour.

Prophets still declare
"Peace will never be gained through
Massive violence"

Judas with other
Agents of bloodshed have their
Places in history

Bombing will destroy
Both body and spirit of
Nations dropping them*

* "Some of us were beginning to hope that…we were ready to accept the peace ideal, to recognize that the man who cleans a city is greater than he who bombards it, and the man who irrigates a plain greater than he who lays it waste" ("Democracy and Militarism," speech by Jane Addams, Chicago Liberty Meeting, April 30, 1899).

Poisoning of Earth
Will continue until we
Step forth in protest

There is no such sin
As spiritual gluttony
In seeking our God

Terror as tactic
Will not frighten anyone
Always doing good

With oceans rising
Our Earth warming steadily
Other matters pale

Earth is our sole ark
Apart from which we won't find
Another refuge

Earth's Plimsol measure*
Is evident to prophets
Who are not well liked†

* Economist Herman Daly writes of the Plimsol line on hulls of ships that take on cargo. If the ship goes deeper than the line, it is in fact, sinking.
† Ecological economists who seek a reduction in profit-seeking at the expense of Earth are rejected by government officials and CEOs who seek limitless growth. Those who disregard the ecological prophets and economists are willing to sacrifice future generations for short-term profits.

Nations are hijacked
By brazen wealthocracies*
Trashing our planet

* Citizens of East Liverpool, Ohio, lost a twelve-year battle to block an incinerator from opening near a school. Teri Swearingen was one of the leaders in the futile effort to protect children. She was given the Goldman award for her part in the struggle. In her acceptance speech she said: "We are now living in a wealthocracy where it is corporations versus Earth, government versus the people and 'experts' versus common sense."

Finding bliss in prayer
Is God's deepest desire for
All who seek union

Life on volcanoes*
Demands readiness always
To exit our homes

* Winnie Bacque, an airline stewardess from Lafayette, La., had lunch with a prominent woman from Paris in April 2002. Mrs. Bacque asked the elderly woman, a survivor of World War I and World War II, for her opinion on the present moment in time. Without hesitation, the senior woman said, "We are living on a volcano."

Rising from the dead
Implies leaving graves of our
Former addictions

One who is truthful
Will not always gain respect
In times of darkness*

* Congresswoman Barbara Lee (Dem. Calif.), referred to above, has come under attack for being the only one of 435 representatives and 100 senators because of her opposition to massive military retaliation in Afghanistan. Thereafter, she received over 2,000 death threats (The African-American Community after 9/11, C-Span, February 23, 2002). The United States in 2002 is embroiled in military actions in Afghanistan, the Philippines, Colombia, and determined to take the "battle against terrorism" to fifty or sixty nations, according to Secretary of Defense Donald Rumsfeld. In

June 2002, "thousands of troops are now in one-hundred countries," according to National Public Radio.

We have been committed to an endless state of warfare by the present administration. The military-technological-complex will take in billions of dollars in this futile campaign for peace. Rather than bring about peaceful relations with others, our present policies are certain to generate more enemies and drain our own resources.

Scientists warn us
Our history has become
Atomic countdown*

* In 1947 a group of nuclear scientists who were familiar with the dangerous weapons introduced into warfare began a periodical known as *The Bulletin of the Atomic Scientists*. On the cover of each issue they placed a "Doomsday Clock" with midnight depicting the hour of global nuclear conflagration. When the United States detonated a hydrogen bomb in 1953, the minute hand was just two minutes from midnight. In the post-cold war optimism, the hand stood at seventeen minutes before midnight. On February 27, 2002, the hand was moved back to the same position it was in 1947. (Associated Press, February 28, 2002)

Which nation first used
"Weapons of mass destruction"
"To end" a World War?*

* On the contrary, organized mass violence has intensified. The United States and the European Union are the leading sellers of weapons to impoverished nations around the globe.

Lacking safe water*
Will incite more battles than
Petroleum wars

* By 2025 there will be a critical shortage of potable water for 2.7 billion people. A United Nations report, issued through the International Atomic Energy Agency warns of "a looming crisis that overshadows nearly two-thirds of Earth's population" (Vienna, Austria, March 23, 2002).

Voracious deserts
Advance every moment on
Paralyzed Beijing*

* National Public Radio report of March 22, 2002. A "brownout" from Gobi desert sands covering Beijing is a major factor weighing against Beijing's choice for the International Olympics in 2008.

> We prefer to die
> Rather than amend blind ways*
> Fixed in our gross greed

* W.H. Auden (1907-1973)

> Upon growing up
> We might perceive God's plan for
> Our deep compassion

> Our lives are fixed on
> Eternal inheritance
> We can't comprehend*

* "That is why Christ is the one who mediates a new covenant between God and the people, so that all who are invited can receive the eternal inheritance promised to them" (Hebrews 9:15).

> Humility more
> Than money matters to God
> On our final trip

> Mothers do not mind
> Ageing that much if all her
> Children remember*

* Who rememberss that phone call, card, and flowers?

> When violence reigns
> Safe refuge is rejection
> Of any killing*

* Everyone has the right to self-defense, even if it demands killing another person. However, in the strictly pacifist mode, we are not obligated to kill rather than be killed. Each one must consult with his/her own conscience, as did Franz Jagerstatter, the "Saint of Conscience," referred to above, in the twentieth century. For his refusal to participate in the German military, this Austrian citizen was beheaded on August 9, 1943, as "an enemy of the state."

Since our time is short
Do what remains to be done
Now with God's help

Finding time for prayer
Hours at peace in poetry
Are our ecstasy*

* Time of overwhelming joy. In Greek: "standing outside oneself."

Let's think globally
Then act quickly* because time
Will not wait for us

* Variations on "Think globally, act locally."

Your truth, then my truth
Might not be congruent with
God's eternal Truth

In our every breath
You are there to have and hold
For the rest of time

"Make A Way" railroad*
Came about as violence
Was thought to be right

* "Make A Way" is the name given to "railroads" as engines disappeared in the internal war of Sierra Leone (population 5.4 million, average life span 45 years for men, 51 for women). The "train" is actually two men pulling a cart on the rails (National Public Radio, February 28, 2002).

Limpid eyes, guileless
Faces portray God's divine gaze
Without speaking once

"Enronization"*
Will quickly crater all those
Who adore profit

* Enron is an energy corporation based in Houston which collapsed in January and February 2002. The implosion of Enron was followed by a greater collapse of WorldCom in June 2002.

Blind politicians
Are children playing with Gog's*
Nuclear pistols

* Gog and Magog are the two nations that will war with the Reign of God at Armageddon.

By fate we are Earth's
"Last healthy generation"*
Of which we aren't proud

* Conclusion of Sr. Rosalie Bertell, a scientist who has studied the impact of nuclear radioactivity on those born after 1945, the beginning of the atomic age.

Have but one great hope
Being consecrated* in
God's eternal Truth

* "For their sake I consecrate myself, so they too may be consecrated in truth" (John 17:19).

Never veer from Truth
If we desire to remain
In God's loving care

Preachers talk of God
Those in deep prayer go straight to
Our Source of Love

        Any worry is
        Our complete waste of God's time
        If we have deep faith*

* "But you, you must not set your hearts on things to eat and to drink, nor must you worry" (Luke 12:29).

        In the cool of Earth's
        Morning or evening God loves
        Slow walks with each one

        At every moment
        We are being transformed by
        Our God's Holy Breath*

* "I will remove the stony heart from within you and give you a heart of flesh" (Ezechiel 36:26).

        Survival is THE
        Most important spiritual
        Question of our age*

* Never in history has humankind held such a devastating military capacity.

Without Earth healing
Our self-healing* won't begin
On the road to health†

* Hundreds of books along with magazines on enhancement of SELF are available. In the last decades of the twentieth century, a growing number of books and periodicals were published with an emphasis upon the healing of Earth.
† A grammar school girl from El Paso, Texas wrote the following poem:

"I am the ill Earth
People have cut down trees, which are my lungs
They have polluted the streams, which are my blood veins
They have polluted the air, which is my brain
They have polluted the oceans, which are the chambers
  of my heart
My wrath has gotten great
My wrath is hurricanes and tornados
Floods and other disasters
I am the ill Earth
If people trash me, I will die
And so will they"

How rare is our day*
When something never before
Heard enters our ears

* "The greatest pleasure known to us is the discovery of a new thought, the second is riddance of an old prejudice" (Frederick the Great of Prussia, 1712-1786).

Pain for prophets is
Seeing clearly* what others
Cannot envision

* For most of his life, Thomas Berry (1914-), a visionary, geologian, and cultural historian has been warning of the steady termination of the Cenozoic Age.

When our day calms down
Serenades by frogs* lull us
Into deep slumber

* Tropical storm Allison brought five days of heavy rain and flooding to Louisiana and Texas during the first week of June 2001. Thousands of frogs emerged from ditches and pools of water in Lafayette, La., to dominate the evening solace.

Our most beautiful
Moment of every day comes
In contemplation

We are lent bodies
Who allow God's life to flow
Throughout our cosmos

Rise to greet each one
So they will not look down on
Our inertia

When Caesars are wrong
We cannot remain silent
Even behind bars

While we roam in space
From where do we find
Our medications*?

* Over half of our prescription medications come from the natural world. Rain forests now vanishing at a football field per second are the most abundant source.

In sharing their light
Candles do not lose any
Power to give more

Throughout everyday
We strive to reflect God's deep
Loving forgiveness

Globalization
Will be obfuscated by
Earth in rebellion*

* Climate change and global warming (www.climatehotmap.org) are cosmic forces that will gain the attention of CEOs and world leaders who refuse to acknowledge Earth's limitations.

Invasion by cars*
Threatens all who seek pure air
Walking about town

* Over half of each city is occupied by roads, parking lots, and auto-associated enterprises. In Los Angeles, the vehicle occupation is two-thirds of the metropolitan area.

We might like to know
Katydids* are neither birds
Nor blooming flowers

* Katydids are large, long-horned grasshoppers in North America.

By following paths
Planned by The Invisible
We will find our peace

Why is our quest for
Oil, not water the biggest
"Busy-ness"* there is?*

* Exxon made $17 billion in 2000.

God invites each one
"Bloom where you are planted" then
Rely on My love

Global warming will
Affect every creature* from
Now till the last day

* When asked what is the greatest problem facing humankind, the famous anthropologist, Dr. Richard Leakey responded without hesitation – "Global warming." Rejection of the 1997 Kyoto Treaty is an indication of massive denial by the United States, an act of cosmic terrorism that will jeopardize life in the future.

Deep contemplation
Is God's desire for each one
Beginning today

Betrayals teach us
Never to inflict such pain
Upon anyone

Each moment of life
We are basking in God's love
Even when hurting

Our first hour in prayer
Allows the remaining day
To flow in good works*

* BEING is more important than DOING. "Whatever we do is not really that important, but we must do it anyway" (Gandhi).

When will death arrive?
Is our concern prompting us
To finish all tasks

Mother nature calls
Each one of us to kneel down
Then gently pet frogs

Call all "anaweim"*
By warm first names as God does
Since their conception

* The "little ones," insignificant people (in the eyes of the media) who pick up our garbage, wash dishes in restaurants, change and bathe incontinent patients in nursing homes, work for $1 a day in "maquiladoras" along the Mexican/U.S. border.

In just one moment
Sun energy exceeds ours*
Throughout history

* In 10,000 years, including camp fires, coal, gas, wind, nuclear, coastal, geothermal energy, the Sun provides more energy in a second.

Children must be taught
Words over munitions will
Triumph in God's time

Only nature makes
Every snowflake uniquely
Distinct from others

Divine forgiveness
Is certain as Earth's sunrise
Without conditions*

* "As far as East is from West, so far have I removed your sins from you" (Psalm 103). Obviously, there is need for us to reform our errant ways.

Even in prisons
Joyful peals of laughter roll
Throughout dim hallways

When there is no trust
Our best choice is to become
Utterly honest

"Water, water" is
Everywhere we look but can't
Slake our thirsting selves*

* "Water, water everywhere, nor any drop to drink" ("The Rhyme of the Ancient Mariner," by Samuel Coleridge, 1772-1834).

Above and below*
All in the universe pour
Forth in praise to God

* "The spirit of the worm / beneath the sod / in love and worship / blends itself with God" (Percy Bysshe Shelley, 1822-1892).

We don't recognize
Earth alone sustains each one
From day one till death

If each breath is a prayer
Drawn in deep gratitude
What need for words?

In our confused age
Stay close to people who are
Of little account

Women will express
Compassion towards each one
With more ease than men

No matter how fast*
Earth's speed will not cast us out
Into great darkness

* As given above, Earth's rotation speed is over 600,000 m.p.h.

One day Earth will ask
Why do you continue in
Harming both of us?

To where do we flee
When we can no longer drink
Nor bathe in water?

Every burning light
Draws its brightness from one small
Chunk of coal somewhere

Cool breeze under trees
Cavorting squirrels seeking food
Our moment of calm

Dinosaurs teach us
Process what is occurring
For your survival

"I am so happy"*
Sincere words flowing from one
Seeking rest in God

* Last words of Gerard Manley Hopkins, Jesuit poet (1844-1889).

When clothed in great wealth
Flaunting massive kill power
How wrong can we be?

Words require effort
Actions flow with aplomb from
Deepest convictions

We now pride ourselves*
On lives not acceptable
To our mother Earth

* Political leaders in the United States boast of "the highest standard of living in history."

We are all bright stars
Assuming consciousness in
Blossoming bodies

If no life comes forth
Our message is not from God
Who is pure Goodness

Great changes might occur
When we perceive Earth as our
Very own bodies

Earth will not welcome
Another century of
Wanton destruction

We all have the right
To refuse belief in words
From high officials

History makers
Of apocalyptic scenes
Are now in power

Violence put forth
Will of its own nature return
Upon our own heads

Deep contemplation
Will help us stay afloat in
Frequent tsunamis[*]

[*] Japanese for tidal wave.

Let all that draws breath
Now give deepest thanksgiving
To the Source of Breath[*]

[*] "Let everything that has breath give praise to God" (Psalm 150:6).

Vic Hummert

Vic Hummert is from Breese, a small community in southern Illinois that does not have an industrial smokestack and only two traffic lights. There has only been one homicide in the town since its founding in 1856.

From this tranquil, rural, and coal mining background, Vic grew to become a community organizer in Harlem in 1965 and 1966. In 1970 he went to Hong Kong, the world's most densely populated region, for a decade as a missioner-social worker. To obtain a priceless grasp of colloquial Cantonese, the southern Chinese dialect, after eighteen months of studying "proper" Chinese, Vic took a job as a factory worker for the wage of $2.30 for an eight-hour day.

In 1982 Vic returned to do peace and environmental education in the United States. In 1989 he began a program of environmental education in the two most "ecologically disadvantaged" states of the union – Texas and Louisiana.

Since fewer than 5 percent of U.S. citizens do any "serious" reading and very few want to deal with the overwhelming information regarding environmental decline, Vic chose the haiku, written in defense of nature, as a terse medium for raising public awareness.

Vic and his wife Roselyn now live in Lafayette, Louisiana, a city of 108,000 people. Roselyn serves as a chaplain in the local Catholic hospital. Vic is the chaplain in Lafayette's county jail, with a "parish" of nearly 800 residents. "It is the best parish of my thirty years as a priest."

978-0-595-43780-1
0-595-43780-X

Printed in the United States
74627LV00004B/382-480